I Am So Done With You!
A Men's Dating Guide to When to
Break Up With Your Partner

By Liam Carson

*"The dating book for men
that women need to read!"*

I Am So Done With You!

A Men's Dating Guide to When to
Break Up With Your Partner

By Liam Carson

*"The dating book for men
that women need to read!"*

LOVESIP
PRESS

Table of Contents

Introduction

This book was simply written because of a need. The unspoken truth is...men need help with relationships too, and while this is a book intended for men, it is one that women need to read as well, for it will surely benefit *both* sexes.

With the advent of social networking sites and dating apps, the number of people that are breaking up today is staggering! While this book may aid and abet those numbers, clearly, it is an indication that the right men just aren't finding the right women, or vice versa. It may also be a result of misplaced values. Perhaps those people who are breaking up could have stayed together if only values were in their proper place. People seem to be getting together more and more, for the wrong reasons, often originating in greed, selfishness and material desire. Or, they break up for the same reasons. Unconditional and unwavering love does matter more than anything else, and people need to once again realize this, and take the time to find it, otherwise there is the risk of an empty and hollow existence – not to mention, societally, an empty and hollow future – a vastly unfulfilling prospect in the end, when, at 87 years old you may have dentures, *Coke* bottle eye glasses, and be sporting a new pair of *Depends* – love better be there!

This is not a book of misogyny, nor was it written with misogynistic overtures and intent, however, undoubtedly, as is always the case in this modern era of 'attack first, ask later', some will scream that it is indeed a book of misogyny. To them I say, "I'm sorry if you feel offended," but let us take a moment and count the male-bashing, feministic, female relationship, chick-lit, female instruction guides, groups and movements that concurrently exist in our society. I might also add that if any woman sees a reflection of herself in this book, then perhaps you need to reassess and undergo some improvement yourself, at least where relationships are concerned.

Is it a balanced playing field? If it was balanced, neither sex would need help at all, but the reality is the antithesis. Droves of people continue to search and seek counsel on love, relationships, and dating. I continue to hear stories from both male and female friends that still point to the perplexing condition that the "good" guys still cannot seem to find the "good" girls, and again, vice versa. Yes, it is a two-way street.

As there are men who are dopes, jerks and selfish, cold-hearted, bastardly cheating fools, so too are there women of the same measure. This book is merely an aid directed to help men against the latter group. Touché.

-- Liam Carson, August 17, 2016

The Moment Before:
Your Pre-Game Speech

If the book's title caught your attention and you are reading this sentence, then you know exactly what this book is about. This book is designed to create and bring about a healthier and more enduring relationship, the irony is, it may not be with the one who is in your life right now!

Just what are the grounds for the dismissal of your significant other? What are the signs to break up? What are the reprehensible offenses? This book hopefully provides the answers to those questions; it is a guide to help you decide when to tell your partner to, *get the hell out of your life!* Besides, some people need it told to them.

While this book is results-oriented, it is not about getting "the upper hand" in a relationship, but rather getting what is best for YOU! It is about what you should tolerate and what you should not, ultimately leading to a better self and a more hopeful and positive future – the wellness of a life. Someone once told me that after every relationship you learn something new about yourself, and I have found this to be true. It may require quiet reflection and remembrance, and it may not become evident until a healthy amount of time has passed, but if you look or examine hard enough, it is there. It is our indicator of growth; of relationship enlightenment! And if you believe in fate, any one relationship may be – or may have been – the requisite for the next great one that lasts forever.

I am an advocate of equality and harmony in a relationship – equitable benefits for *both* sides, but this equity seems to be lost, with most relationships in a constant state of imbalance. While there are almost always an array of relationship hurdles to overcome, making it feel like an obstacle course, military basic training or a labyrinth sent from relationship hell, there are and should be an abundance of benefits and rewards to be received, and often, what you put into it, you will indeed get out of it! Frequent minding and maintenance of your relationship will almost always reap a harvest – unless you are simply with the wrong person! That's the rub. In our rapidly changing technological society, we now find ourselves in a day when the male-female playing field is as volatile as ever. However, as there are well-defined parameters for women, there ought to also be the same for men, to help determine just how much you should put up with...and whether you are with the right person.

So...here's that convenient compass to guide you through the nebulous relationship jungle. It should help you to answer an all-important question that was the title of a hit song by *The Clash*, in the 1980's..."Should I Stay or Should I Go?"

Now, read the rest of this book and then go do what you have to do – or not do. Either way there are only so many tomorrows, and life is too short to wallow in a relationship that has a broken future. If you are ever feeling like yours is broken or if you are drowned in misery with the walls closing in, you now have a guide to determine whether you should do something about it.

(There is one disclaimer to this book: I want to again make it *very* clear that all relationships operate from two perspectives. Men can be deceitful and abusive jerks too. Before you spring, be sure *you* are not guilty of the same faults detailed in this book – unless of course it is obvious that you both bring out the worst in each other, otherwise known as a destructive relationship that serves no one. Relationships always require work from *both* parties, along with a healthy dose of self-assessment, so you might improve yourself as a person to the point that it subsequently fosters the relationship. Be certain to carefully consider all of the mitigating circumstances and try your best not to be partial only to yourself – as I will reiterate later in this book, applying mutual consideration and empathy can go a long way toward bringing harmony to a relationship.)

When to Break Up
With Your Partner

1. **If she cheats on you**, even once, tell her to get the hell out of your life and do it fast! The sooner the better, and avoid the muddy, drawn out speeches, even your breath is suddenly too precious to waste any more of it on her. Regardless of the circumstance under which it happened, cut the string and move on. You will forever have a glowing reason why you left her. You must ask yourself: What does this mate now offer that another cannot? Nothing! If you are reading this and you have already caught her cheating once and taken her back, you best have eyes behind your head because chances are exceptional it will happen again. Respect plays a major role in this latter scenario; the majority of women have more respect for a man who exhibits strength in matters of this nature and responds appropriately, rather than a man who hides behind his own fear of

---

All farewells should be sudden, when forever.

-- SARDANAPALUS

loss and sheepishly accepts what has occurred; actually tries to understand the rationale and excuse given. In short, don't be a wimp or you'll end up being walked on forever, never to be looked upon with regard by your mate again.

2. **If she tries to entrap you**, lies about a pregnancy that never was, bilks money for a dream that was never conceived or cons you about a sickness or disease just to keep you around, tell her to get the hell out of your life, and don't fall for the "play of pity" that she will inevitably perform out of desperation. She may even threaten suicide if you leave – another entrapment.

This is not a relationship, it is a delusional arrangement concocted by a cracked mind or sinister heart. She thinks nothing of playing Russian roulette with your life, derailing it into some awful state. Do not waste time trying to seek revenge or discussing the matter, in an attempt to acknowledge the reality of the situation, for it is impossible to reason or elicit any form of rationale from a deranged persona. Has there ever been a successful negotiation with evil? A soul that resorts to entrapment is a member of the lowest grade of humanity – get rid of her! Let the ending credits roll! If you invest any trust in

---

I don't want the cheese;
I just want out of the trap.

-- SPANISH PROVERB

these types of women you are bound to be continually bitten – and doomed!

3. If your mate has a chemical imbalance and is on prescribed medication, and she did not tell you about it, she may never be forthcoming about anything else that may arise, or perhaps there are other secrets. It thus becomes an issue of honesty and trust, a tremendous risk when you consider the ramifications of an "ever after". Why does she feel the need to hide anything from you?

Did she wait until after you were engaged to tell you about an anxiety or mood disorder? Did she tell you that it was a mild case when it was actually severe? Or did she tell you that she was only on 10mg of Zoloft and you learned that it was actually a much higher dosage? These are all huge red flags! They can also be premeditated elements of deception. If any of these examples apply to you, walk on. The future suddenly becomes too uncertain. As unpredictable as your mate is, so goes the relationship. You are not here on this earth, or in this life, to save anyone – unless of course you woke up one morning and discovered wings behind your shoulder blades and a halo over your head!

---

please
close the door
gently as you go

-- ALLAN TATE

The only disclaimer to this rule is if the relationship is still "new"; less than six months old, in which case you still don't even know the woman, and thus at such an early stage, it is difficult and ill-advised to hold her accountable or cast blame for lack of any personal disclosure. We are living in an age of 'Big Pharma' drugs. They are everywhere, but it doesn't mean you should settle. Truthfulness in these major matters should be part of the foundation of any healthy relationship.

4. **If your mate craves status or comes from a status-driven family**, is only concerned with image, treating your relationship as if it were a public relations agency, tell her, "Goodbye!" She will be forever plotting your life for you and you won't even know it. In the end, you mean nothing. The kind of car you drive, the house you buy, the clothes you wear, and what others think of you, have more value than any love you will ever offer. Thus, you become a heartache waiting on the sidelines of some ever present field of misery – the fresh air of life and love blows not here, only lavish country clubs, VIP passes, foot races with the pseudo-rich, and BMW lease agreements reside here. The flowers cannot sway in the breeze because they are fake and ornamental, with no roots born from

------

Get your tongue out of my mouth,
I'm kissing you good-bye.

-- CYNTHIA HEIMEL

the underneath – just like your relationship, shallow and without natural substance, teetering on stilts in the open sea. Do you want to live a life that is a total façade? Are you being true to yourself? What matters more to you, a life of status…or a life of love and longevity with someone who would stay with you through a depression – if all you had were the clothes on your body and a humble abode?

5. **If she spends your money faster than you do. . .** umm, "hello?" Do I really need to justify this one? Okay. Even though this happens a lot in today's twisted version of a society, it's not right and it's not good. Even if she is a supermodel and you have great sex! If or when you run out of money, chances are great she will run out too. And don't bother putting your running sneakers on – she's gone! The alternative: Should she not leave you or decide she'll try to stick around, she would have to change and alter her lifestyle to a more affordable, practical version. Do you really think that is going to happen? Should we consult with an odds-maker in Vegas? Save yourself the trouble. Tell her, "goodbye", and to take their $4000 to $5000 per month spending sprees elsewhere. You are far better off pampering a dog. If you have worked damn hard earning your money and you pride yourself on sen-

---

It's the good girls that keep the diaries;
The bad girls never have the time.

-- Tallulah Bankhead

sible practicality – an admirable, responsible, and noble trait – then you don't deserve to be with anyone unappreciative, mindless or careless. I am not advocating "cheapness", but there is a world of difference between spending money, and spending money in excess. A healthy relationship is being with someone who possesses a similar system of values, and who is with you because of YOU, not because of your money.

6. **If your mate is a "gold digger"** or you suddenly have a revelation that she only wants to marry you for money, get rid of her faster than the moldy food in your refrigerator. Unless of course you are a gold digger too, in which

---

There once was a woman named, "Bitch",
Who spent his money like she was rich.
From 9 to 5 she played,
Except for a coffee when she was delayed.
Furs, jewels and a dog named, "Sue"
Suits, boots and make-up too!
She kept an eye on "Rex" –
who drove a Porsche and liked rough sex.
She hadn't a job,
Work made her sob.

She came home one day to her man named, "Ray"
Who sadly admitted, "I can no longer pay."
His pockets were empty, the mortgage was due,
She grabbed the last diamond and away she flew!

case you're made for each other. Otherwise, love remains the necessary ingredient to any healthy, long-lasting relationship, not money. These gold-digging arrangements never work in the long term, they are empty. How many different ways can you spell, "D-I-V-O-R-C-E"? Dump her even if the sex is really good. Smarten up! That's her hook! Sex! And she knows it. After all guys, it has been said that, "One hair from a pussy can pull a freight train," and that's a quote attributed to a woman – Joan Rivers! Do not ever think that a woman does not know where her points of power, persuasion and influence are. I once overheard two young women talking in a bar:

"Oh, he's so hot."

"Yeah he is, but does he have any money?"

"Are you kidding me? Of course he does or I wouldn't be with him. He drives a Lamborghini."

"Oh my God, you're so lucky. Keep him as long as you can!"

And then of course there are some New York City women who, when I lived there, wasted no time in asking me what fast became three of the most famous Manhattan questions, always asked within 60 seconds following introduction:

Nothing is more dreadful than a cold, unimpassioned indulgence. And love infallibly becomes cold and unimpassioned when it is too lightly made.

-- ALDOUS HUXLEY

1) "Do you live here in the city?"
2) "So what do you do?"
3) "Do you have a car?"

Naturally, if I did own a car at the time, that would mean I was fairly well-off, since I'd have to afford *two* rents – one for my apartment and one to park my car!

There is one caveat to this rule. If, while with your significant other, you suddenly strike it rich or find yourself swimming in wealth, and you notice your mate thoroughly enjoying the riches too – it does not make her a gold-digger, nor does the newfound money give you license to look where the grass might be greener and search for someone perceptibly better. If she was supportive of you up to the attainment of the wealth, share it with her. Allow it to enhance your relations, not destroy them. Remember, when we die, we take the love and the affection that we feel with us; the intimacies of wisdom and the breadth of heart that was bravely invested in others; we take the care and the sanctity for life – all of those days of sun and laughter that did not wither the love in our souls, but illuminated and enlivened the hearts and lives of others; that made the tastes of life sweeter. We take with

––––––––––––––

Don't go with girls you'd be ashamed to marry.

-- JOHN UPDIKE, Couples

us the joyful extremes of our senses, not the material wealth and bounded worldliness of money.

7. **If you give your girlfriend flowers and she puts them aside with flagrant, un-appreciative carelessness**, break up with her! I can attest from experience that this ungrateful act leaves a raw feeling on your innards, as if someone just scraped off some precious material. Chances are very good that you have a spoiled and ungrateful wretch on your hands. Who gives a damn how pretty she is! Give her the boot! You will never be able to make her happy. These types have no regard for the thought or the trouble you may have gone through to get the flowers.

Usually, these types of women have never had anyone tell them *it's over* – so be the first, it's about time they got their first life lesson. There are some exceptions to this rule: Some women either do not like flowers or are allergic to them. I was even with one woman who flat out told me, "No, don't get me flowers. They're dead in less than a week. It's a waste of money." If any of these exceptions apply and you still bought her flowers, then you are either inattentive or insensitive – and the fault is inevitably yours. Another exception to this rule is if you

---

A great many people fall in love with or feel
attracted to a person who offers the least possibility
of harmonious union.

-- RUDOLF DRIEKURS

have been a total asshole, and you think flowers might redeem you or put a bandage on your crappy behavior – umm…no.

8. **If she misses your birthday and flat out fails to acknowledge it,** tell her to get the hell out of your life. You should not always expect to be the first thought on her mind, or even the second – life gets busy, but if she totally overlooks the day that you came into existence, you need to drop her from your future plans. You are dating a self-absorbed, oblivious or cold-hearted ghoul! What would her reaction be if you forgot or failed to acknowledge her birthday? God forbid! And aren't relationships supposed to be reciprocal and equal? Birthdays are important. Even if you are miles apart on that special day, a video chat and/or a phone call are the least requirements.

There is one exception…ever see the movie, *The Devil Wears Prada*? When Anne Hathaway's character misses her boyfriend's birthday because of work, but still does acknowledge it, but the boyfriend is still pissed? Well, if your girlfriend is an ambitious career girl and misses the party because of career demands, but does acknowledge you while apologizing for not being there, you've got to respect her. 'Cut her some slack' and let it go. Be proud of

---

'Tis good to be off wi' the old love
Before you are on wi' the new.

-- RICHARD EDWARDS

her accomplishments, which could mean the world to her. I am definitely an advocate of career pursuits and career demands that face men and women alike, and so should you. Mutual support goes a long way in a relationship.

9. **If she steals from you,** forgiveness is not even an option. Get the hell away from her and do it now! Before you know it, she'll be stealing from your mother...or your dog! If she has already stolen from you or from others, and you are still with her, you are immediately entered into the "YOU'VE GOT TO BE KIDDING ME" category.

Theft is not a mild offense; it's one of the *Ten Commandments*! Moses even waved the heavy tablet over his head and cried, "Thou shalt not steal!" You do not want to be with someone who requires you to have eyes behind your head or sleep with one eye open. You do not want to be associated with someone who is engaged in criminal behavior. Can you really envision your life with a thief? Waking up next to one, smelling their thief-like breath? If you give them your love, they might steal that too – along with your sperm, your kidney, and your car keys to get away! If it is a sickness, then offer to get her help and then get the hell away from her, and as you drive away, start humming the *U2* song, "Walk On", with a big smile on

---

There is more self-love than love in jealousy.

-- FRANCOIS LA ROCHEFOUCAULD

your face, happy that it's over! And umm…same goes for you – if you're a thief without a conscience, expect to be dumped. In my adult life, I've come to the conclusion that thieves are the least desirable people on earth – which includes some politicians.

10. **If she does drugs and you do not,** or if she was hiding her drug use and habit from you until you found out, get rid of her. What if you want a family? What if the habit worsens and the results spill into your home or worse, involve your extended family? What if it is a hard drug habit like cocaine, heroin or crystal methadone, the latter of which has claimed thousands of lives in recent years? What if there is a debt to pay to a drug dealer? (No, it's not far-fetched, it happens every day.) Are you pre-pared to protect your family? Your partner? Are you willing to raise the stakes and risk your life and to face danger? Do you have the money to bail her out of trouble? Or jail? Are you emotionally equipped to deal with the countless mornings of despondency, and mental and physical erosion; mornings when you long for the company of a trusting friend because of the raw, unfor-

---

I loved thee once, I'll love no more,
Thine be the grief and is the blame;
Thou are not what thou wast before –
What reason should I be the same?

-- ROBERT AYTOUN, To an Inconstant Mistress

giving emptiness she has bestowed upon you? If you stay with her, chances are good that an easy moment and a cup of coffee with simple sunshine streaking through the kitchen window, will be a distant memory. There are far too many "what ifs". Get her help and then softly tell her that you no longer wish to continue the relationship; if you do not, brace yourself for likely hell – tranquility will fast seem like an unattainable dream.

11. **If she is an excessively jealous person** to the point where it impedes and weighs down your life, then give her something more to be jealous about – your freedom. Life is too precious to have jealous limits thrust upon it. Examples of this would be anger and jealousy every time you meet new people, or give a friendly greeting to a total stranger or even those you already know; jealous because of your success or the attention you may receive; jealous because you had a more enriched upbringing (even though you now share it with them); or jealous because you are close to your mother or father, which she perceives as a threat to her ideal kingdom (which is also evidence of a "control freak"). Jealousy is a malady. It can eat away at a conscience and destroy a relationship. Jealously

---

A competent and self-confident person is incapable of jealousy in anything. Jealousy is invariably a symptom of neurotic insecurity.

-- ROBERT A. HEINLEIN

is a sign of insecurity, and thus your burden. It can crowd a mind, create awkward moments in public, and strain your communication with family and those close to you. Being with someone who is jealous requires you to give them constant attention in an effort to reassure them – only they will never be reassured, no matter what you do. Not now. Not ever.

Those who are jealous also have a tendency to exhibit passive aggression. They may even demonstrate acts of malice because they want you to pay for their own feelings of jealousy. So...if you have a mate who exhibits jealousy daily, or on a regular basis, tell her to get out of your life – you simply don't need a person like that, and when you are rid of her, you will feel lighter, and see the beauties of life more clearly, actually experiencing the sensation of a life without restrictions, released from the jealousy that inhibited you and prevented you from living! Cheers!

12. **If your significant other embarrasses you or 'cuts you down' in front of others,** if she insults and criticizes you, that is a sure sign to give her the walking papers. This type of behavior could reveal a plethora of personality flaws, the most obvious of which is cruelty. Others include coldness, disrespect, inconsideration, spite, cyni-

---

Here is the door, and there is
the way, and so...farewell.

-- JOHN HEYWOOD

cism and…a complete and utter bitch! If you stay with this type too long, your image – and perhaps even your confidence – will suffer a devastating blow. You'll be left trying to figure out or understand why she acts in such an evil or humiliating way, and when you confront her, she may blame you! YOU make her act that way! Get away from her before she dismantles you completely. One maxim you must always put into practice in this life, to enjoy a fruitful and healthy existence is: Avoid all negative *people – avoid them like the plague!* Their negativity is not only contagious; it's harmful to your health.

Some people are just downright mean. They litter the earth like useless fodder, causing storms wherever they go. No woman is worth this pain and humiliation, and the one who is, won't make you feel this way or have you on constant guard. Your psyche should not be torched with critique, or put ablaze by perpetual scorn. A healthy relationship should be like a cool, fluttering breeze that brings solitude and wholeness to your heart and soul; in between the squabbles, it is the acquiescence of your most private thoughts with theirs, continuous moments of the most

---

How strange to have failed as a social creature — even criminals do not fail that way — they are the law's "Loyal Opposition," so to speak. But the insane are always mere guests on earth, eternal strangers carrying around broken decalogues that they cannot read.

-- F. SCOTT FITZGERALD

fantastic and wondrous dreams, where everything is always the first time and holding hands is like making love.

13. If your mate continuously nags you despite your requests to stop, break up with her! All women nag to some degree, as do some men, but being overwhelmingly nagged is like having a dagger forever thrust through the gelatinous membrane of your mind, resulting in a harrowing existence that makes you wonder if you should have taken that job shoveling shit in China – it is also damn exhausting! Do not the existing demands of life and work make you tired enough? Have you any desire for peace? Nagging often occurs in those people who are excessively demanding, controlling or high-maintenance. Should you remain with them, your life will fast become a "nit-picked" and "hen-pecked" mess; a "life of conditions" and you will be reduced to a fragment of the man you once were, because you will either turn into a submissive wimp who falls into the habit of saying "yes, dear" all the time, just to get her off your back, or you will drive yourself crazy trying to get away from her, inclusive of extensive bathroom stays, far beyond the time required – forever trying to be in a place or room where she is not, even if it means hiding in a small box with the dead mouse your cat dragged home.

While we are postponing, life speeds by.

-- SENECA

You will often observe similar behavior in the way her mother treats her father. It doesn't go away. Tell her to get the hell out of your life, and just like that, she hasn't anyone to nag!

14. **If she frequently exhibits bizarre behavior** like the proverbial "wigging out for no reason"; if she screams at the top of her voice because you drank the last glass of wine or put a footprint in the "just vacuumed rug"; if she makes a scene at the restaurant and flips out on the waiter because they can't accommodate one of her many requests, or if she suddenly starts throwing eggs at the neighborhood squirrels – if she is vastly irrational and "throws a fit" over 'nothing'…tell her you are done with her or your moments of peace will be few, and your life will fast become a dungeon (and I don't mean whips and chains, think more along the lines of an embarrassing hell). I once had a girlfriend who mistook the bathtub for the wastebasket. The tub was on the left and the basket was on the right – she must have been partial to her left – I'd find used tissue near the drain. Then there was the woman who used so many hygienic sanitary wipes when she went to the bathroom, that she clogged my toilet – repeatedly. When I nicely tried to suggest that she please use

---

Your old-fashioned tirade – loving, rapid, merciless – breaks like the Atlantic Ocean over my head.

-- ROBERT LOWELL

something else or a different brand...she started taking them out of the neat, little, pink plastic box that stored them, one at a time, and threw them at me in anger, until the box was empty and they were all strewn about the floor! I started seeing red. Not in rage, but as in a BIG RED LIGHT!

"Caution! Caution! Possible whack job in your house!" I calmly picked up the towelettes off the floor, took the opportunity to clean some dust while I was at it, poured some wine, watched a re-run of *24*, and waited for her to leave. I put some fast space between us, and didn't make any more plans with her for the rest of the week, and then I broke it off the week that followed. My confirmation? She ended up calling City Hall and told them that there was something wrong with the sewer system AND my toilet. She complained that my commode did not meet specifications. City officials came knocking on my door soon after. When I explained to them who was probably behind their visit, they left laughing and told me my toilet was just fine.

With these types of women...what if something really legitimate did arise? A major issue of contention or a high-pressure situation? A terrorist attack that required you to turn into Jack Bauer from the television show *24*,

---

Look in my face; my name is Might-Have-Been;
I am also called No-more, Too-Late, Farewell.

-- DANTE GABRIEL ROSSETTI

in order to save the world? What coping or conflict resolution skills have they to rely on? Will they have the capacity to calmly arrive at a solution or compromise without bringing down the roof...or jeopardizing the operation? I don't think so.

15. If your significant other is emotionally unstable; she cries for no apparent reason or gets depressed and blames you for it; she becomes reliant on you for her happiness and tells you that if you leave her she'll kill herself – rather than wallow in guilt or pity, get her help and then get the hell out of it! Do you know what it's like to have your finger in a vice? Get stuck with this type and you'll have an idea. This rule bears some resemblance to the "bizarre behavior" rule above. I was once getting a body massage from a very intuitive and wise woman who was also practiced in Reiki energy healing and crystals. While she was massaging my back, she suddenly said to me, "You just broke up with someone who was dear to you, didn't you?" I said, "Yes, how did you know?" She answered, "Because the muscles behind your heart are very sensitive and there is a buildup of energy there. Your heart is aching." She then uttered a quote that I would never, ever forget. She said, "Always remember, *Saviors get slaughtered and Martyrs get punished*." I tell you this be-

---

A new love drives out the old.

-- FRENCH PROVERB

cause it is very easy to fall into the trap of trying to save the emotionally unstable; trying to understand their actions and thought processes, but if they don't understand themselves, how are you going to understand them? This is not an exhibition of cold-heartedness. You simply may not be equipped to be with them. Wish them well and have sympathy for their emotional plight, but move on. They are on their own path in this life, and you have to stay on yours.

16. **If she confronts you with issues that are absolutely off the wall,** or if she gives you an ultimatum that has no basis in logic or reason, while ignoring foundations of love and affection, do not delay, break up with her and tell her to never contact you again! I once had an ex say to me, "Okay, I have three issues: Kids, Stability, and Seat Belts." Seat Belts! I wanted to tell her to go get a job with the Department of Highway Safety! I asked her if the seatbelt issue could be a deal breaker, to which she replied, "Potentially." I asked myself, is this how shaky the foundation of our supposed love is? How insincere her love is? She'd break up with me over a damn seatbelt!

Issues that "come out of nowhere" are often born from selfishness and from extensive conversations with those

---

Love knows not its depth until
the hour of separation.

-- KAHLIL GIBRAN

close to her. You have to understand, for some women love is only a line drawn in the sand, their investment is as deep as the tip of their finger. Logic tells you it is only a matter of time until the line dissipates, erased by a simple wind. Your heart unfortunately tells you otherwise, it only knows how to give of itself. However, as hard as it may be, get away from these fleeting souls before it is too late, lest your heart be in danger of breaking in two. As it turned out with me...the seatbelt issue was indeed an indication of her insincerity. We were done for good a week later, and looking back, I swipe my brow and say, "Whew!" Words cannot express how glad I am that she is not in my life.

17. **If she insults you and degrades who you are**, with comments like, "Well, now that I've thought about it, if we have kids I might want to stay home with them and I won't be able to do that on your salary alone." (Subtext: You don't earn enough money for me.) This was actually said to me by a girl who was bringing $70,000 in student loan debt and a car payment to the relationship table, while I hadn't any debt at all. At the time, we had been to-

---

Oh, seek my love, your newer way;
I'll not be left in sorrow,
So long as I have yesterday
Go take your damned tomorrows.

-- DOROTHY PARKER

gether for more than a year and I was in graduate school, working as a substitute teacher while I completed my coursework for my Master's Degree. That night I postponed all of our future plans.

If she insults you and thinks nothing of it, degrading who you are as a man, your livelihood, career pursuits and personal makeup – all of which this particular woman mercilessly went on to do – you simply don't need her. You may have simply had the bad luck of getting stuck with a spoiled, selfish, disrespectful bitch, like I did. Get rid of her fast and tell her to GET THE HELL OUT of your life with frosty fervor. (In this instance you are allowed to substitute "hell" with some other expletive for added measure.) They deserve it.

Why have such shallow, transparent women in your life, who curse and bite the hand that feeds them? Go find someone who appreciates who you are and what you have to offer, and is not solely concerned with their security and your ability to take care of them.

18. **If she is overly flirtatious with your friends or other arbitrary men,** to the point where it could be per-

---

Do you know what it means to come home
at night to a woman who'll give you a little love,
a little affection, a little tenderness? It means you're
in the wrong house, that's what it means.

-- GEORGE BURNS

ceived that she is cultivating affection, attention or an affair, and despite your pleas and requests to stop, she persists...break up with her, or she'll drive you nuts. She may be a woman who enjoys and thrives on creating jealousy – or at least trying to create it. She may also do it because she needs constant attention or she wants to be certain that she can still flirt with the best and be the center attraction, which is a sign of insecurity. It all spells trouble for the relationship. You will find yourself having to baby-sit her whenever she is in the company of men, or if you turn away, you may feel the need to have one eye open behind your head. Another result could be the ruination of your friendships should an extracurricular affection develop.

If you are with a woman who makes constant overtures to other men while you watch – you'll look like an ass without a backbone. You will be talked about – *Did you see how she was all over me right in front of him?* And people might think you're dating a whore! When you break up with her, beware...the first man she calls might be your best friend. The one way in which this type of be-

---

And I shall find some girl perhaps
And a better one than you
With eyes as wise, but kinder
And lips so soft, but true
And I dare say she will do.

-- RUPERT BROOKE

havior is acceptable, is if you are both swingers, or perhaps you have an 'open relationship' and there is mutual consent.

However gentlemen, be sure you are not overreacting or being overprotective; that you are not treating your mate as if she were a piece of property that you own! (Whenever I see a guy being overly possessive of his girlfriend, or being physically or egotistically dominant, I want to smack him!) Also, be sure you are not guilty of the same offense, being overly flirtatious with *her* friends. Gallantry and self-dignity are admirable attributes – practice them.

19. **If your mate is making a pointed habit of kissing work colleagues on the lips** at Christmas parties, functions or other events when greeting or leaving, and she refuses to stop, citing the lame excuse of possible demotion or the risk of offense, tell her instead to take all of the men in the back room and have at them, because you're leaving. It is inappropriate and a complete measure of disrespect, and a huge red flag, not to mention a potential

---

It may be true of all relationships,
not only between fathers and sons, but
between men and women. Nothing seems fixed.
Everything is always changing. We seem to have
very little control over our emotional life.

-- SHERWOOD ANDERSON

breach of trust. It may also be indicative of a reckless and careless persona – one who simply "cruises" through life, damaging hearts as she goes, purely for the sake of advancement. She doesn't give a bloody damn about you, like you thought she did. Unless – again – you and your partner enjoy the swinging or kinky lifestyle, these are not harmless kisses. Does she find it so enjoyable kissing her colleagues that she cannot simply turn her cheek? If she respects you then she ought to respect your wishes when you ask her to stop. After all, a healthy relationship is two hearts interwoven. If hers is entwined with yours, why would she want to kiss the lips of any man after you asked her not to? Another consideration: what do you think is going through the mind of the colleague she is kissing? Do you think he or she is saying, *oh, how flattering, she just respects my work?* No, they're likely thinking how they might be able to squeeze a couch from IKEA into their office by next week, or the location of the nearest "unknown" hotel, to get some fringe benefits!

20. **If your partner is passive aggressive** then break up with her. You can double the severity of this offense if they exhibit the passive aggression toward your mother. This rule may also apply if you have witnessed their

––––––––––––

Better never to have met you in my dream than
to wake and reach for hands that are not there.

-- OTOMO NO YAKAMOCHI

mother and family member's passive aggression. The apple never falls far from the tree and that sure isn't any tree you want to climb. If you don't tell her to take a hike you'll be the constant victim of passive aggressive behavior for something you did two weeks ago – forever! Or even worse, you'll be forever wondering what you did wrong.

There was once an ex who was exhibiting passive aggressive behavior toward my mother. For two weeks I pressed her, politely asking what was wrong. Finally it spilled out. She was angry that my mother bought a dress that was seemingly so similar to her mother's dress, that she found it offensive. *SO THERE! IT'S OUT!* was the subtext of her statements and subsequent attitude. My reply: "You've got to be kidding me!" Passive aggression often originates from a pile of petty bullshit or, it is the result of the aggressor's poor communication skills. There are no guarantees it can ever be fixed, especially if it is genetic!

21. **If your mate is disrespectful to your parents for no apparent reason,** tell her to take a hike. If she respects you, she ought to respect them. Is it worth mediating warring families for the rest of your life? Or forced to choose sides? Arguments will forever abound. The disrespect may also be stemming from jealousy or some other deep

---

What is evil? – Whatever springs from weakness.

-- Friedrich W. Nietzsche

rooted issue or baggage. The disclaimer here is if you yourself have had an altercation or major issue with your parents; if there is a valid reason for the disrespect or tension. Your mate may simply be acting out of love for you, so be certain and be sensitive to this possibility, so you can make the proper call.

Remember, a relationship is a rhythm, you have to work to keep it alive; you have to communicate. When the rhythm is broken, well...think of smelly socks in your tuna salad. What feeling instantly surfaces in your stomach with *that* image? Isn't that what it's like when a relationship isn't going smoothly? You get sick to your stomach and dread having to deal with it or confront it because you know it could bring more conflict. Everything is uncertain and the uncertainty controls your every thought and rules your day. A broken rhythm in a relationship is like a pestilence, if you don't make adjustments and cure it, it will get the best of you. If you don't confront the disrespect...expect a broken relationship rhythm.

22. **If your mate is utterly absurd!** This is related to the bizarre behavior rule, but "absurd" and "bizarre" carry different extremes. The Scribner-Bantam English Dictionary defines absurd as: "ridiculously unreasonable", with synonyms such as "foolish, wild and nonsensical." Does this

---

A love that goes awry can become one of the most haunting memories of a life – or lives – if you let it.

sound like someone you are with? I had an ex who did not want me to see a movie because it showed a lack of control by the female lead character over the man – she didn't want me getting any ideas. The movie was Cinderella Man. She "dissuaded" my viewing of it after having already seen it without me. This is an example of absurdity. Her mother probably warned her, Don't let Liam see this! It shows the man in control of his own destiny and he ignores the wishes of his wife – plus he can barely provide for her! If you have an episode that matches or tops this one, I can tell you that it is indicative of your mate's cracked and outrageous view of the world and your relationship; it would serve you better to buy her a Cuckoo Clock, help her hang it on the wall and then leave! These types just haven't a clue about life and you may find more peace in a sanitarium.

23. **If she deceives you in any way, look out!** If she 'pulls a stunt' like leaving your parents off the wedding invitation after it was already mutually agreed to put them on; or tells you she is going to meet friends for her book club or go to Chicago for a business conference, but you find out she instead met an old boyfriend or would-be boyfriend for coffee, or went to a gay club with intentions

---

I finally had an orgasm and my
doctor told me it was the wrong kind.

-- WOODY ALLEN

of a one-night romance; if she suddenly turns on you and decides to change her mind about how she feels; if she knows you are on a tight budget and you come home from work and find the house or apartment redone with new furniture because, "that's the way it was on HGTV," and her mother told her to, "get rid of that crappy-looking, old furniture," or if you told her intimate secrets that you did not want anyone else to know, and she spilled them to her friends, your neighbors, your work colleagues or someone else...all of these examples are grounds for dismissing her from the relationship. In a committed relationship, you are both supposed to be on the same page of life, considerate of each other. The old word for actions like these is double-cross. It amounts to a sly and careless unpredictability in your significant other that you must not endure. Women can be a lot like water – if the water is murky, don't drink it!

24. **If your significant other has a meddling mother who sticks her nose in the relationship and all affairs concerning the relationship;** if her mother wields her influence behind the scenes and floods your mate's head with total crap and your mate hasn't the guts to take control of her own life and to tell her mother to "back off",

---

Eyes, look your last!
Arms, take your last embrace.

-- WILLIAM SHAKESPEARE, Romeo and Juliet

you better end the relationship sooner than yesterday. You might as well be in bed with her mother while her daughter watches.

I was once with a woman who did not act on her own volition. I should have known better when, after she and I agreed to explore an outdoor marriage next to the water, she went home to discuss it with her mother. The following day the idea was completely "off the table" and out of the question. Her mother insisted that her thirty-year old daughter was not to be married in that manner – no, this did not occur in India as part of some arranged marriage. My fiancée simply obeyed, without a fight and without any consideration for me. This same mother even scrutinized my wedding invitation list and it is the same mother who caused a blowout when she *felt* that my mother's wedding dress was too similar to her own – without ever laying eyes on it! The only similarity: spaghetti straps. Yes, petty bullshit, but any defense was useless. Needless to say, the marriage never happened. When a mother has this much control of her grown child's life, run fast! Actually, run faster than *Forrest Gump*, with a smile on your face that you're escaping a life

---

Just remember the world is not a playground but a schoolroom. Life is not a holiday but an education. One eternal lesson for us all: to teach us how better we should love.

-- BARBARA JORDAN

of horror...and a would-be mother-in-law whose knife is still in your back!

25. **The 'Bitch Factor'.** Okay guys, a little is expected, even a lot is tolerable so long as it's not 24/7. If it is 24 hours a day, to the point where even your friends can't stand her, tell her goodbye – you may want to call her a Bitch! Or tell her to Screw! Although she may interpret the latter as a command or invitation, and before you know it, you'll be locked in heated passion – perhaps the most heated you've ever had, and a sense of bliss may overcome you, and you may start to have second thoughts about leaving her, until she rolls over and says, "Why do you always have an orgasm before I do – and don't answer that because I'm tired of your fucking excuses. You forgot to pick up my dry cleaning, now go take out the trash!" I find it amazing that some women act as though being a bitch is part of their repertoire, their responsibility in life; I'm a woman, so it's okay if I'm a bitch...no, no, wait a minute...I have to be a bitch!

I have heard many women say, "I just want a nice guy," but when they get one; when they have a man who is

---

People have to talk about something just to keep their voice boxes in working order, so they'll have good voice boxes in case there's ever anything really meaningful to say.

-- KURT VONNEGUT JR.

sweet to them, cooks for them, loves them, is sensitive and considerate, they turn cold as ice on a dime – the obligatory bitchiness just pours out and spills everywhere, like...like a broken relationship that springs a leak and shoots out leftover bitch-words on those moldy love notes. Life is supposed to be happy. Life unimpeded really can be good and rewarding and wonderful. Who the hell would want to ruin that prospect of wonderment by living with a bitch? Her mood alone will kill your flowers, ruin your TV shows and...and...spoil your food! B-Bye!

26. **If your mate is a compulsive liar**...this is a very, very sticky rule that in a number of instances beckons mercy on your behalf. The key word is "compulsive". White lies are excluded; everyone lives in some sort of concocted reality, one that carries elements of a wrangled imagination, after all, our lives, whether you are aware of it or not, are created by our thoughts, desires and imagination. However, what I am referring to here is the incessant, habitual liar, as well as those lies that hide pertinent or key relationship issues. No healthy relationship was ever based on lies. No love was ever built on deception. Since a harmonious, healthy relationship is like a well-built house, it re-

---

Women marry men hoping they will change.
Men marry women hoping they will not.
So each is inevitably disappointed.

-- Albert Einstein

quires and begins with a solid foundation. What kind of a foundation do you have if it is infested with lies? What trust? Sincerity? Love?

Like termites, lies eat away...eating at the nucleus of the relationship until it crumbles and disintegrates. Some people like to lie. They enjoy stretching the truth and embellishing a story. For some, if they get away with the small lies, they'll try on bigger ones. You must be keen; there are some very good liars roaming around out there.

The parameters for what lies are grounds for dismissal are actually quite nebulous or indistinct. Why? It is unfair to demand or expect a woman to divulge a past failed pregnancy for instance, or perhaps an abortion. They are painful memories and after a time, they are memories that the body buffers from conscious thought. They are not pleasant or desirous recollections. To ask a woman to re-live a painful experience is not a fair proposition. Some women have also been victims of horrific hate crimes, crimes of passion, and other traumatic experiences. They must not be expected to be forthcoming with you about everything, not right away at least, and thus, the longevity of the relationship does play a significant role here; empathy and sensitivity on the man's behalf best be summoned and exercised.

However, if they are lies that deal with seeing past boyfriends, husbands, drug use, sexually transmitted dis-

---

My father gave me some advice,
"Never try to win the same girl twice!"

eases, entrapment, theft, criminal behavior, malicious intent or habits that can become pitfalls in a relationship, such as addictions or health issues; lies that equate to deceit or attempts to manipulate you or those close to you; lies that are selfish and self-serving that cause hurt and heartache...then get the hell away from them. If she was your pet snake and she said she wouldn't bite, would you believe her?

27. **If your significant other calls you or text messages you every 20 minutes while you're at work,** to the point where it jeopardizes your job and your ability to function, but she just doesn't get it or care to get it; if she doesn't give a damn how it may be affecting your career, tell her to get the hell out of your life. She is acting out of pure selfishness, inconsideration, cluelessness and disrespectful obsession. This also falls under the 'nag rule'. Let me guess...whenever you show any frustration over her constant calls, her response is, "I need to talk to you," and that's that! No...Bullshit. Buy her a book on independence, and if she has that much time on her hands, she ei-

---

"You gave me the key of your heart, my love;
Then why did you make me knock?"

"Oh that was yesterday, saints above!
And last night – I changed the lock!"

-- JOHN BOYLE O'REILLY, Constancy

ther ought to get a job, get another job, or get a more demanding job that pays more. These types of women may never leave you alone, and it also may be a sign of that most fearful label, "high-maintenance". When you get fired because of her, she will still expect you to take her out to dinner. Say, "Bye-Bye", and change your phone number.

28. **If your significant other has you followed;** if she hires a private detective or trusted friend to trail you, and there is absolutely no reason for it – you have been completely faithful and have given no signs to make her think otherwise – then tell her to get the hell out of your life. Your mate is suffering from psychotic paranoia. Buy them a copy of One Flew Over the Cuckoo's Nest, and leave. This is an indication of excessive mental baggage; deep-rooted fears, insecurity, and anxiety with which you will never stop wrestling and attempting to ease the subsequent impact on your relations. Before long, she'll have a spy program installed on your computer to trail all of

---

Though his suit was rejected,
He sadly reflected,
That a lover forsaken
A new love may get;
But a neck that's once broken
Can never be set.

-- SIR WALTER SCOTT

your keystrokes, have your phones bugged, and put a nano camera in your bedroom! She'll go high-tech on your ass! You have to understand...paranoia is a thing that only grows – it gets worse, just like your life would if you don't end the relationship. And yes, of course she'll deny having you followed! See Rule #24 on "compulsive liars" if you need further justification.

29. **If you have a partner who is only in the relationship for her own advantage,** kick her out of your life – not literally, she'll call the cops. She is not with you for you; she is with you for what you can do for her! It might be for status, money, career, clothes, image or even revenge on a past love. Hopefully you'll be smart enough and have the awareness to discern this, because the only question she will ever ask is, how can this benefit me? In other words, she doesn't give a cow's ass about you. A woman without a heart is never worth having – not ever! Even if some prior actions revealed a trace of one; in retrospect you shall find that those actions were purely mechanical, almost robotic, and in the "I'll do this because this is what I'm supposed to do" category, just so she could snag you – or snow you. It really depends on how you wish to see it, but know that you have been snowed,

---

Love is a fire. But whether it is going to warm your heart or burn down your house, you can never tell.

-- Joan Crawford

like a freaking blizzard that freezes your heart. How cunning of her. Now it's your turn. Dump her! After you do, she may reflect on how nice of a guy you really were and come crawling on hands and knees. And what if she does? I still wouldn't take her back! No! No! No! Too big of a risk and you don't know the sincerity of her actions. You have to protect your heart!

30. **If your partner is unable to make key decisions on her own (also see "Meddling Mother");** if you learn that she always runs to her mother or sister or friends for counsel, it is a sign of instability, immaturity, and perhaps insecurity. Get out now! These types of women run from themselves and the truth. There is a high probability that your mate has a history of going through men like water without any emotional closure, which is actually an unnamed relationship syndrome. Why does she act like this? How is she able to do this with such ease? Because all of the decisions that were ever made in past relationships were not her own, thus resulting in less emotional investment; others made the hard decisions for her. She may have been coddled and protected her whole life. She may

---

Abandon me to stammering, and go,
If you have tears, prepare to cry elsewhere -
I know of no emotion we can share,
Your intellectual protests are a bore.

-- THOMAS GUNN

never have experienced any consequence for her actions. She sees nothing wrong with jumping from man to man – leading them on, saying all the right things, and then withdrawing without notice.

Beware of these indecisive types, for their family influence is strong and far-reaching. Your mate is a wild card, prone and liable to shock you with a sudden withdrawal from the relationship that will leave you gasping for air and vastly angry, only to later be left reflecting upon how foolish you were to not realize you were dating or engaged to a drone – as in automatic pilot! These women are dangerous emotional traps. Look out!

31. **If she abuses your loyalty and love;** if she becomes ungrateful and unappreciative (she probably always was) and you conclude that she is clearly thinking of leaving you; if she thinks nothing of what you have invested in her or the sacrifices you've made just for her – and if you made them because she conned you into believing that there was some wondrous eternity with her – kids, picket

---

I still could not picture it all taking place on the desk. There didn't seem to be enough room for a woman so tall. I have since discovered that a thimble is room enough when they really want to, and that the whole planet itself may prove too small when they really don't.

-- JOSEPH HELLER, Something Happened

fence, family parties, growing old; if she thinks nothing of the love you shared or the moments that composed it (the love was probably insincere and fleeting on her behalf anyway), and she doesn't give a damn about hurting you, then give her some help with the decision and break up with her. You'll be doing yourself a huge favor. She's just not for you. She probably does not know what love is, and she is someone who is greatly careless with other people's hearts. There are no benefits in staying with someone who has already begun to float her scent in the direction of other options or contingency plans involving other men or perceived opportunity. Someone better awaits you. There are degrees of ungratefulness that are virtually sinful, never mind cold-hearted. Thank your stars above for having enough foresight to end it sooner than later, and if you don't, I hope you like torture...as in having your heart put through a meat grinder.

32. **If your mate pays little or no attention to you or frequently ignores you,** and even though you spend half of your days with her, you feel like you are spending them alone – you might as well have the company of an ant as it traverses the landscape of a wall. Let me guess: she pays little attention to your romantic overtures too! Find some

———————————

After three days men grow weary of
a wench, a guest, and rainy weather.

-- BENJAMIN FRANKLIN, Poor Richard's Almanac

self-respect and give yourself more credit! Pack your stuff and get out. What a waste of life! You'll get more attention at a nursing home, helping and conversing with the elderly – they'll appreciate your company and you'll attain great positive karma for the good deed! They'll even return your phone call! This woman is not for you. You are not for her. Move on! Why stay in it? Comfort and convenience?

These excuses reflect the tyranny of the weak; this is your life, and you haven't the time to be weak. Is it possible to dance the tango with a 120 pound lead weight? Try it with your girlfriend who ignores you and you'll have a fast clue of how it would turn out. A happy, healthy relationship should be like a hill in the country or a sprawling field, where there are nothing but carnivals, ballgames, cotton candy and apple pies; summer dresses and bow-ties! Elation abounds, the sun is always shining, and the soft blowing air is crisp…and temperate for love.

33. If she bitches and bitches and bitches… bitches about the color of the sofa; bitches about the way you shut the door; bitches that you get home too late; bitches that it's your turn to get the milk; bitches that you didn't call her back fast enough; bitches that the dishwasher leaves spots on the glasses, and the kicker…bitches that she

---

Parting is not sweet sorrow but a dry panic.

-- JOHN STEINBECK

wants kids, but then bitches that you work too much – beware! She may even be the worst of all bitches: a bitch of entitlement! She thinks she's entitled to everything without doing anything!

If you do have kids together, she will be complaining about them too, even though she wanted them more than life itself; even though she wanted them more than that ever-elusive, eternal, infinite orgasm! After she does have her children, she will still be complaining that you work too much while demanding that you take the kids 'off her hands', like they're a piece of bad property, so she can do Pilates or Yoga. She won't care that you provide the family income because that's expected. You are so better off to break up with her now, before it escalates into a horrifically miserable scenario, one that has you staying at work even longer to avoid facing her. Upon your exit, the words "spoiled", "ungrateful" and "clueless" should be central themes in your farewell oration, and oh yeah..."BITCH!"

34. **If she is never happy with you, no matter how much you do for her** – no matter how much energy you exert, to the point where you find yourself exhausted; no matter how much you try and make her feel like she is the hot fudge sundae of your life; that she is the Swiss Alps,

---

Who ceases to be a friend never was one.

-- GREEK PROVERB

and a never-ending vacation in Burmuda, and despite this, she still suddenly springs on you:

a.) "I don't know what I want" or
b.) "I feel like I'm on the sidelines of your life."

Both of these lines or anything similar, are absolute warning signs. The first is an example of a woman who is either a complete jerk, a complete fool, or someone who indeed does not know what she wants, which means she's either led you astray or you've misread her and have been 'spinning your wheels' for nothing; either way she is un-predictable and thus a gamble, and maybe you're just not meant to be with her. The second statement is an example of someone who is very insecure, mentally unstable, or a control freak because she can't seem to harness you – or she is all three of these. Break up with her and do it quick because her eyes and mind may have already started to look elsewhere, far beyond you. Do not let your heart get completely trampled by someone unworthy of having it in the first place.

These types of women will never be happy, and may in fact be happier being with a complete and abusive asshole because they'll never be given the room to think about whether the relationship they are in is good for them.

Keep your bitch on a leash!

-- "Andy" 40 Year Old Virgin

35. **If you suspect she might be gay when you're straighter than a speeding bullet,** well…you better get to the bottom of this one and fast. If you confirm that she is indeed gay with absolutely no further craving for the male penis, unless it is packaged in latex or rubber or glass or hard plastic replete with a one horsepower motor, or attached to a belt or harness…well guys, take it on the chin because there is no longer much use for you now is there? For some men, this is a blow to their ego and pride. Do not let it be. It does not mean you are insufficient or a lesser man. This life is about choices, desires, wants, needs, and also temptation and discipline. The situation in which you find yourself is actually a reflection of our present world society. Freedoms are exercised more freely. It could be perceived as an act of carelessness and inconsideration, with casualties of deception in the wake. Choices and decisions are made every day in this life – some of them quite damaging. You must flat out admit that this person simply is not for you and you have a concrete reason – they're gay! Big deal. Get over it. So what. Perhaps they always were, but didn't know it. Frankly, bring yourself to supporting her lifestyle decision, it will be easier on all parties. Would you really want to stay with

---

To meet, to know, to love – and then to part,
Is the sad tale of many a heart.

-- SAMUEL TAYLOR COLERIDGE

her and continue to live a lie to your friends and family? Would you really want her to be in a relationship that she no longer wants to be in? She'd be faking a whole lot more than just orgasms! Wish her well – sincerely – and be on with it.

Hopefully you found out before you got married and if you didn't, then yes, it is a very big deal, in which case you must work diligently to end relations with swiftness and realize that you have your life ahead of you. She is not who you thought she was. She may have not been honest with you. She may be mentally unstable – which has nothing to do with her being gay. There may have been no way for you to have known. Hell, she probably didn't even know! This type of situation occurs more often than you think. Some couples try and stay together as swingers – I do not advocate nor advise this latter practice for it can be an empty, loveless, emotionally punishing relation-ship – a reality significantly left-of-center!

If she is wavering and saying something like, "Well, I'm just not sure if I'm gay or not. I like being with women, but I just don't know. Maybe I'm bisexual. But I don't get anything out of sex with you anymore." I'm sorry, but you should still end it, unless of course you think you might

---

It is seldom indeed that one parts
on good terms, because if one were on
good terms one would not part.

-- MARCEL PROUST

be bisexual or have bisexual tendencies, then maybe you might be able to exist in some kind of synchronicity.

However, if not, then DO NOT entertain they're indecisions because it is your psyche that is at risk of being damaged. In these situations you need to look out for yourself. She may want to remain friends, but at first you should probably resist if there is pain and agony involved; cease all communication, move on and do not look back, otherwise your head is liable to be a trophy for the insane – you'll end up driving yourself nuts trying to figure the whole thing out, the "why's" and "how's" of it all, and it's just not worth it, and far too risky. Erase her from your life, and move on. Maybe you can be friends later, after you've moved on, both mentally and emotionally. Life is not without its detours...and remember, you are never alone when you have to take one.

36. **If you discover that your significant other has been maintaining a "hidden" or ulterior lifestyle – a double-life – and she either kept it from you for an extended time or you found out by accident,** show her the door and break up with her. This also falls under the categories of "lying", "deceit", "distrust", and "disrespect", amongst others. Ulterior lifestyles can become extremely

---

All's over then: does truth sound bitter
As one at first believes?

-- ROBERT BROWNING

dangerous contingent upon who is "dragged" into it or already involved. Forms of desperation can manifest in the people that she is involved with in her ulterior lifestyle, whom you likely know nothing about; they can likely be characterized as "sketchy" or "seedy" in their appearance and daily behavior. Desperation can also suddenly become apparent in your partner. It is simply not worth even trying to work through it – your mate is already gone! She's already been swept up in her other life, and you're not included or welcome in it! Before long, you'll probably be living a secret and making excuses to your family and friends because of her behavior and absence. Whether the ulterior lifestyle involves drugs, sex, crime, or some form of role play, it is not to your advantage to try to understand it. Absorb the shock and move on. She is simply not who you thought she was – not anymore.

37. **If you are treated like some career trophy or an equestrian stud,** just because you would be a good breeder and yield some handsome babies, tell her she might have better luck with a horse and end the relationship promptly. The bottom line here is that you just don't matter – who you are, what you represent, your entire make-up, persona, values, goodness, and kindness; your

---

Great spirits have always encountered
violent opposition from mediocre minds.

-- ALBERT EINSTEIN

character traits, talents and skills – it all amounts to a nocturnal emission in the eyes of your girl...you know, a wet dream? And how fast do we forget those dreams? As soon as they dry up! All that matters to her is your ability to give her a good-looking baby or babies along with some stability from your perceptibly stable job. Don't forget that a large percentage of women only want to be taken care of; they want you to alleviate their familial and financial insecurities and anxieties. In this instance it is only about what *she* wants and thus you subsequently become an integral part of her objective, not a relationship. If she suddenly perceives that you will fail to offer her the stability that she so selfishly desires, she will drop you faster than the thought of her next prospect or conquest – you know, that guy in Chicago or Delaware or that Army officer who will submit to any pretty woman; who she can shape and mold and train? The fundamentals of love are

———————————

Since there is no help, come let us kiss and part,
Nay, I have done; you get no more of me
And I am glad, yea glad with all my heart,
That thus so cleanly, I myself can free,
Shake hands for ever; cancel all our vows,
And when we meet at any time again,
Be it not seen in either of our brows,
That we one jot of former love retain.

-- MICHAEL DRAYTON

not a priority to her. Where does a girl most often acquire such an objective or idea? Where else? Her mother!

38. **If the formalities of a wedding trump, supersede or overrule your relationship;** that is to say if, what has become the institution of planning a wedding becomes more important than you, your entitlements (being half of the overall whole) and the consideration of your desires; if the foundation of your relationship, its nuances, reasons for love and mutual moments shared are suddenly overlooked and you become just an insignificant "extra" in the planning of the big event...that's a big red flag. It is simply not fair, courteous or considerate. It's just not cool! It is your day too! You and whatever sacrifices you made need to be considered, whether you wish to participate in the planning or not, and it absolutely does NOT matter who is paying – it is your day as well. Without you, would there even be any planning? It should be a day that encompasses the compromise of both of your lives – a combination of both your tastes, whims and delights. It should not be a one-sided affair nor should you be relegated to 'by-stander status', with strings pierced into your mouth, pulled to open by your in-laws, just long enough for you to say, "I do!" If your partner resents you for voicing an opinion or for being critical of any part of the

---

A fresh love sweeps the dust off of a heart,
Gives it some new red paint,
And makes the scars of yesterday a bit lighter.

planning, or she takes offense to your words, and she is not willing to bend an inch – you have a problem.

Once upon a time there was a man and a woman who were utterly and completely in love. They shared everything tender, and professed everything eternal. When they snuggled on a couch it was like Heaven came down and resided within the cushy confines of their embrace. He cooked for her often; she doted on him with endearment and with occasional, soft surprises. Harmony filled the recesses of every passing moment. They yearned for another in absence and rejoiced in each other's presence. She was Catholic. He was raised Protestant, but was unaffiliated. Relations progressed into an engagement to marry. Soon after, the planning commenced. Her mother wanted a big, lavish wedding. He wanted a small, inexpensive one, and would rather spend the excess money on a future house. Her mother insisted they get married in a church. He was not at all opposed to a church; he believed in God, but her mother wanted something for the society pages. He didn't care if it was in the cartoon pages; he just wanted to marry out of the purity of love. The mother insisted. He relented...for *her.* Then her mother wanted money for the wedding. He refused. It was not his preference. He said, "Why should I pay for something that is not my choice?" They moved on. She asked him to partic-

---

Nothing is ever like it used to be.

-- MALCOLM S. FORBES

ipate in the pre-marital activities of the Catholic Church. He obliged...for *her*. She scheduled Pre-Cana. He got formally baptized so to be recognized by the Catholic Church. They met with the priest. They went to the classes (even though he was missing *Sunday NFL Gameday)*. He only fussed. Hours and hours of Catholic obligations fulfilled...for *her*. They started to plan the readers. She said they also had to be Catholic. He asked why. She said that's the way it is. He wanted his minister to read. The minister was not allowed because he was not Catholic. She hired a vocalist, who also turned out to be Catholic. He wanted his brothers – his wedding party – standing beside him when he got married. They were not allowed. He started to protest. She said that's the way it is. He said this isn't only your wedding. She said you're not the one paying for the wedding. He said, my family is paying for the Rehearsal Dinner and offered to pay for half of the invitations. She said, you knew it was either a Catholic wedding or nothing. He said, no, your mother said that; I want my minister to do a reading. She said, he can't. He said, why aren't you hearing me? She said, what do you mean, you keep throwing the Catholic thing in

---

Oh, seek, my love, your newer way;
I'll not be left in sorrow.
So long as I have yesterday,
Go take your damned tomorrow!

-- DOROTHY PARKER, Godspeed

my face every chance you get! He said, you're not hearing me, I'm trying to tell you to consider me here, this isn't only your wedding, and it's my day too. She said, but you knew it was a Catholic wedding or nothing – and you're not the one paying for it. Then, suddenly, her mother criticized his wedding invitation list. He said, why? She said, my mother wants to know who the guy with the P.O. Box is, why is he on here? He said, it's none of her business, but he's an author, and I don't appreciate her scrutinizing my list; I told her I wanted a smaller wedding from the beginning. The argument escalated. He said, why is the wedding planning more important than our love – than us? And why is your mother so involved when it's not her wedding? She said, because my parents are paying for it, plus, she said, your mother can never do any wrong. He said, what has she done? She said, her dress is too similar to my mother's. He said, you've got to be kidding me. She said, no I'm not kidding you. He said, who cares, what's most important is that our mothers are going to be there, plus who's going to be looking at them anyway since all eyes will be on us? She said, I find it offensive. He said, the dresses are completely different, your mother is just mad that mine bought it from the same

———————————

Relationships are like glass. Sometimes it's better to leave them broken than try to hurt yourself putting it back together.

-- ANONYMOUS

store. The differences mounted. The love shook and rumbled, running in streams down the mountainous collapse of a union. He postponed the wedding when she started with an onslaught of petty issues.

Riddled with shock, she withdrew. He asked for the ring back. THE END.

The planning of a wedding can single-handedly ruin what was once a very good thing...or it can save you from a potentially very bad thing! Do not let this happen to you. Talk it out – ALL OF IT – every detail beforehand, before you even engage her! If you start to sense that this scenario could happen to you, run for your life, and while you're running tell her to stay the hell out of it.

39. **If you feel like you keep getting "interviewed";** if you are being treated as though you are a key component on a resume, "Okay, I have three issues. Kids, stability and seat belt," but you have already discussed kids; they know the stability of your career or impending career after college or graduate school, and well, a seat belt? As I men-

---

Your true jilt uses men like chess-men, she never dwells so long on any single man as to overlook another who may prove more advantageous; nor gives one another's place, until she has seen that it is in her interest; but if one is more useful to her than others, brings him in over the heads of all others.

-- ALEXANDER POPE

tioned earlier, this was one I had sprung on me, and she said it was a potential deal-breaker! It's pure drivel. Bullshit. Flummery. What about her stability – oops, I mean *in*-stability? She might as well break up with me because I like *The Wizard of Oz*! Guys, tell your interviewing girlfriend to get the hell out of your life. You need a relationship, not an employer, plus it is a wholly cold-hearted, methodic, robotic and emotionless way to go about communicating. She's so damn selfish she thinks the world was created just for her. Go find yourself someone who is more worthy because in this instance, you might as well date a robot who won't be constantly asking, "So how do you feel about..." as though she is screening candidates.

I know of a cowardly and bizarre woman who, before she was married or had kids, had a serious sit-down with her boyfriend and asked, "I need to know how you feel about a vasectomy. Would you be willing to have one after we're finished having kids, for birth-control, because I don't like condoms?" How does anyone answer such a question and issue that is still several years away from

---

Oh Charles – a woman needs certain things. She needs to be loved, wanted, cherished, sought after, cosseted, pampered. She needs sympathy, affection, devotion, understanding, tenderness, infatuation, adulation, idolatry – that isn't much to ask Charles.

-- BARRY TOOK and MARTY FELDMAN,
Round the Horne, BBC Radio, 1966

being confronted? Sure, go ahead and take the joys out of everything before that. Can I please enjoy my relationship, marriage, and kids first? Yes, it was another relationship implosion, and for him, one happily disposed of. You have no right to be put through such questions. It's *not* all about them. That's not planning – it's self-obsession and craziness!

40. **If she suddenly stops living the life that you thought (and she professed) defined her** – it was her passion, her lifelong ambition, her dream job; she was the happiest she could be when she was doing it, as if she sat naked atop an ice cream sundae with gobs and gobs of sweet whipped cream and velvet clouds overhead – suddenly she uses YOU as an excuse to quit. She quits her job or her professed passion, becomes lazy and spends your money, while basking in fine soaps, fine perfumes and un-motivation. Nope. Uh uh. No way. Not today. Not tomorrow. Forget it. Tell her, "Goodbye". She may be a phony and/or she just thinks she doesn't have to work anymore and you're going to like it – and if you don't, too bad. She also must suffer from the illusion that she's not expendable. So you come into her life and all of her career

---

My wife has a slight impediment in her speech.
Every now and then she stops to breathe.

-- JIMMY DURANTE

passions are suddenly gone? No, unless her passion is as thin as paper.

If in this modern society women want the male/female playing field to level, then they should be expected to pull their weight too, as long as they can, instead of mooching off of you, especially in this volatile economy. She may have duped you, and in fact she could be a woman who only wants you to take care of her. Also read the rules on "equestrian stud/career trophy" and "self-advantage", and then tell her to get out of your life. You may soon find yourself having more respect for dung – there are primitive tribes in this world that use dung and feces as a hair fixative!

41. **If you already know that her mother is a gossipy, "talk-behind-your-back", "scheme-behind-your-back", status-driven annoyance in your relationship,** swamping your mate's head with petty, materialistic, nit-picking bullshit, and odd topics of discussion seem to be injected into your conversations, as if someone told her to say it; if you already know the mother is a phony and you will be living under her thumb as much as your own girlfriend's if you were to get married; if you inherently sense whenever you walk into her mother's house that you've been talked

---

A great part of this life consists of contemplating what we cannot cure.

-- ROBERT LOUIS STEVENSON

about, and when you leave you just know it will happen again – end it! Your girlfriend will become her mother – if she is not already, and if you don't get out now, she will soon start creating insignificant, matter-less issues that will have you wishing you were in one of those *Southwest Airlines* commercials, "Hey, wanna get away?" Only it may be too late. Don't you really wish that you could be a fly on a wall – just once...or twice?

42. If she complains about the sex... there are several degrees to this category and for starters, if she complains that you don't have enough sex together or about your premature ejaculation or about the way you perform, but she does nothing but lay there like a dead clam and only moans for effect, and she is as adventurous as a game of cribbage; she claims she likes foreplay but hardly ever engages in it and fails to be the first to ever initiate anything – ever! This inevitably leads to 'High Stakes Sex', nothing doing but the actual act. No crescendo or even innuendo! No pre-play, foreplay, post-play or even instant re-play!

The modern erotic ideal: man and woman in loving sexual embrace experiencing simultaneous orgasm through genital intercourse. This is a psychiatric-sexual myth useful in forcing feelings of sexual inadequacy and personal inferiority. It is also a rich source of "psychiatric patients."

-- THOMAS SZASZ, The Second Sin

And yet, she expects you to be the next 'Boy Wonder' and last as long as the first quarter of a football game! BUL-LETIN TO ALL WOMEN: YOUR SHARE OF SEXUAL INITIATION COUPLED WITH LARGE DOSES OF FOREPLAY MAKE MEN LAST LONGER! It's the 'relaxation factor' – that process of getting blissfully, hopefully mutually lost in the moment.

If, after sitting down and discussing ways to fix it, (i.e. an added investment from her and perhaps a visit to the local adult shop) and she still complains, tell her to go find someone else, but remind her that John Holmes is long dead and not yet cloned. If you stay with her, in time, the sex complaints will be insignificant compared to all the other complaints she'll have – the sex will become the lightning rod to her eternal bitching!

Gentlemen, for some reason women often feel that they are absolved of any blame in the sex department, not all women, but most. This is where the *Yield* sign stands: If they are not happy with you sexually, surely their eyes and/or minds will start to wander away from you in due time or, their incessant complaining will result in absolutely no sex at all! In this latter scenario, you'll both lose because your basic levels of intimacy and bonding will

---

The people to fear are not those who disagree with you, but those who disagree with you and are too cowardly to let you know.

-- NAPOLEON

suffer or suddenly disappear altogether and you'll be left in a cloudy pool of bitter occasions, snappy dialogue, and not a single gratifying orgasm.

I have also noticed amongst some women the complete absence of sympathy for schedules and careers. They haven't any sympathy for exhaustion or career burdens that weigh the mind, or as an example, perhaps you may be in graduate school while you try to hold down a job, plan a wedding, and pursue a career. They simply want you when they want you and that's that! They expect you to submit to their whims; to have life and all of its securities placed in their lap, inclusive of the satiation of their sexual appetites, without ever having to do much in return – but they'll tell you they are doing a great many things! These types of women will only bring more exhaustion to your already busy life and make the origination of a simple thought a weighty chore.

Then there are the women who play with and use the psychological side of sex to their advantage – sometimes unconsciously. They will complain about the sex, but it really isn't about the sex. It is actually about something else, some other major issue lurking at your bedside. She's not happy about something, and she won't admit it. She uses sex as her passive-aggression. Meanwhile you're left

———————————

Sex: the thing that takes up the least amount of time and causes the most amount of trouble.

-- JOHN BARRYMORE (attributed)

feeling like a crumb; some under-performing stallion who has been made to feel like you have no business even looking at a vagina let alone touch one!

Lastly, there are those women who claim to hold sex on a pedestal; who stress its overwhelming importance and will, for a time, complain about it, and then, suddenly, cease their complaining and *WAHLAH!* sex is really not as important to them as their stability, which perhaps they perceive they have secured because you may have responded to their incessant complaining.

Regarding sex, gentlemen, absolutely be sensitive and empathetic to her needs, and always try to please her (sex should be mutually pleasing and reciprocal), but just keep your guard up when you're in the pre-marital or dating phase. Don't get sucked into the trance and temporary sensation of the sexual orgasmic moment. As I said earlier, women know what powers they have. They know sex can be their 'hook'. It is their cloak and dagger, for behind the sexual veil may lie a very insincere or manipulating woman.

43. If she wants to see a relationship counselor before you are even married – this is an easy one. A no-brainer. If you need to see a counselor now, what do you think

----

Love is a torment of the mind
A tempest everlasting.

-- SAMUEL DANIEL

you'll need later? How about a divorce lawyer? If it's bad now do you *think it will be better after you're married?* Respectfully tell her, *thanks for offering to try, but no thanks,* and end the relationship. You will be benefiting *two* lives – yours and hers, saving yourselves from marital death and misery where pangs of regret and court proceedings will riddle you into numbness for an unspecified duration.

I strongly suggest ceasing all communication with her for at least six to eight months because there may not have been any major blowout in the relationship, but simply irreconcilable differences. If you maintain contact and communication, you may be tempted to resume relations or fall back into the same old routine because it is the comfortable thing to do. Resist, stay apart, and perhaps you can resume contact when you have a clearer perspective, and you realize how ridiculous it would have been to seek that counselor before you tied the knot. Change is good – especially in this instance!

44. **If your partner often has violent episodes or resorts to them during arguments** – if she throws objects at you, especially large or expensive ones; if she makes your friends, family and pets flee the premises or run for

---

Nothing is a waste of time
if you use the experience wisely.

-- AUGUSTE RODIN

cover; if she falls into irrational fits of rage; and if you are not the violent type, tell her to enroll in an anger management class and to get the hell out of your life. If you do not, the violence could only escalate or there may be a more serious medical issue of which you know nothing of. What if you stay with her and eventually have children together? Is that the sort of household in which you want to raise a child? Is that the sort of mother you want your child to have? Also, jog into memory this important tip: If she calls the police and tells them that you are domestically abusing her, regardless of whether she is lying, the police automatically arrest you on the spot and take you to jail. In most states, if not all, on all domestic abuse calls police have to arrest someone, to extinguish the possibility of another episode – they have to separate the two parties. If you can't trust her that she won't throw your family heirloom across the room, how can you trust her that she won't call the police on you, even though *she* is the violent one?

If you are in a situation right now that is already very bad, and you are apprehensive about confronting her, don't even tell her you're leaving – just leave! It's the safer and healthier way to go. In these instances you have to protect yourself. Pack your stuff when she's not home and

---

The best cure for anger is delay.

-- SENECA

get out! If you wait, she may one day lop off your bean with a knife.

45. If she is verbally abusive, especially in front of others, give her the boot. You don't need anyone like that in your life, and if you fail to split with her, you will end up alienating your friends and pissing off your family members, who will want to fit her with a pair of cement shoes and toss her asunder, into the great wide abyss of the nearest ocean, where she can curse your name whilst a shark homes in on dinner. What types of people are verbally abusive? The types that were themselves verbally abused or who came from a broken home or dysfunctional family unit, or perhaps a jealous type who is insecure and bitter in her own skin, or someone who is passive aggressive and allows issues to mount without venting or communicating them; or...someone who is downright classless and in a competition of manners would lose to a cockroach. This kind of behavior may also occur in those people who are bi-polar or manic depressive, in which case they need professional help.

46. If you accidentally (but on purpose) stumble into her email account and find a host of flirtatious emails

---

'Tis sweet to love, but when with scorn we meet,
Revenge supplies the loss with joys as great.

-- GEORGE GRANVILLE, The British Enchanters

from wooing, would-be suitors – and your mate's replies are equally flirtatious or perhaps even suggestive and leading – call her out on it and demand an explanation. If after her explanation you are still suspicious or if she throws a fit because you read their email (which is usually a dramatic act of diversion to avoid the subject), break up with her and let her pursue those *other* prospects. How can you ever fully trust her? In every corner of your conscience you will forever question the veracity of her character, and like a pestering horsefly, it will never go away. The same applies to cell phone text messages, online bulletin boards, or social media posts. It is all equally suspicious and modern day avenues for communicating on the sly.

To some women, men are like shirts, if they see a new or different color they like, an untried color that catches their eye, they want to try it on, mindless and careless of who they might hurt in the process.

Love doesn't have to be perfect. Even perfect, it is still the best thing there is, for the simple reason that it is the most common and constant truth of all, of all life, all law and order, the very thing which holds everything together, which permits everything to move along in time and be its wonderful or ordinary self.

-- WILLIAM SAROYAN

47. **If she only wants to make a purchase or a life-altering move out of vogue or solely for the sake of image,** like having kids (which so many women do – they decide they want a child as if suddenly deciding they want a new couch, not fully comprehending or digesting the social and human responsibility that comes with one), or erecting a salon in your backyard (even though she has no experience), or getting breast implants, *just* to "keep up with the Joneses", and you are not this type of person, get out of it quick, because if you do not, the relationship will fast become one of denial and an incessant string of wants and needs; a façade with no substance, littered with bloomless flowers and vinyl shoes. What a waste of time *and* life! Go find someone with more integrity and sincerity. Go find someone more real! You're almost better off with a cadaver!

I have a brother who one day bought his family a Yorkshire Terrier puppy. The next week his neighbor's wife bought a Yorkshire Terrier. Then my brother traded in his pick-up truck because it kept stalling, and got an SUV. The next month, his neighbor bought an SUV. My brother and his wife enrolled their children in sports and

---

There is a false modesty, which is vanity;
a false glory, which is levity; a false grandeur,
which is meanness; a false virtue, which is hypocrisy,
and a false wisdom, which is prudery.

-- JEAN DE LA BRUYERE

activities. Suddenly, you'll never guess what his neighbor's wife did, (I bet you can write the next sentence). If your mate has this problem, get rid of her. It is a very expensive habit – it is *The Epidemic of Falsitude* and it occurs in the land of pitifully demented minds that suffer from reality displacement and often subscribe to the magazine, *Life Without a Clue*. The true essences of life will almost always be absent with these types. Happiness and fulfillment are 'inside jobs', they don't come through possessions, status and money.

48. **If she is overly concerned with how much money you earn,** to the point of needing to know your bonus and raise schedule – that only means she's already planning on how to spend it. In fact, consider your future bonuses and raises already spent, or her actions may be motivated by her need to ensure that she is taken care of and her security "secured". Either way, end it and tell her to go make her own money; love plays second fiddle in her mind and that's reason enough to get out of it. Love in any relationship should be a constant season, not a part-time one. Relationships today are in dire need of rediscovering the core of love – it needs to be the base of every relationship. Not money!

It takes a couple seconds to say Hello,
but forever to say Goodbye.

-- Anonymous

I must frankly admit that I am so fed up with those women who have an obsession with money and finding a man with money; those women who look their prettiest, all dolled up, readily offering sex to secure a fortune. Don't these women understand how tragically thin and transparent such a life is? How worthless? How largely insecure and weak it is? Even within the classrooms of philosophy and theology, these money-driven souls are only bound to return to this life, or one like it, for what have they learned while here? What have they gained that is of worth? What have they taken away? Nothing. They were not seekers of wisdom nor did they seek to nurture or better themselves spiritually and soulfully.

Their lives are cheaper than a *Nickel & Dime* store. It is a sad reality to bear in mind that some women only marry for the riches and spoils, *and* the alimony. If you read enough online forums for women and listen to their conversations, this truth becomes crystal clear. Fortunately, not all women fall under this category, but those that *do not* are sometimes difficult to find.

This is also a reason that I am a proponent of women's rights. A 'career-woman', one that is driven and passionate about achieving something for herself, is a good thing. Besides…they have every right to pursue goals and

---

There's nothing sooner dry than woman's tears.

-- JOHN WEBSTER

dreams of their own, and you should both support and encourage it.

49. **If your partner's family is unforgiving, cruel and bullying;** if they are a bunch of sadistic, insensitive bastards, rude and forever insulting or perhaps threatening, and your partner sides with them, leave the relationship immediately! There are already enough assholes in this world, you don't need them living in your house or becoming a part of your family, unless you want to live a life that includes taking idle swings at your in-laws, and politely knocking the shit out of them while saying, "Oh, excuse me!"

If you don't get out of the relationship, tension will build and you might one day snap. Do you get my point? It will happen – you will get sucked right into the vacuum of violence and revenge. Negativity often breeds more negativity. Choose *Positive*, and get the hell away from her *and* her family. Sometimes relationships really are the equivalent of dealing with derelicts or the psychologically insane, and I'd venture to say that certifiable jerks populate approximately 33% of this nation, so you have a one in three chance of encountering one, and if they happen

---

The time has come: for us to part
You're like an old shoe, I must throw away
You're just an old has-been: like a worn-out joke.

-- IDA COX, Worn-Down Daddy Blues

to comprise your partner's family...well then, you're a jackpot winner. Run! Enough said! I don't wish to waste another word on the garbage of the earth.

50. If she consistently shows no shame, no morals, no virtue, no couth, and no hesitancy in incurring hurtful blows to you and others; no heart, no pause in committing blatant and careless acts of malice and deceit or public humiliation, you owe her no explanation when you tell her "goodbye!"

These types will stab you in the back and smile while doing it. Cold, hard cynicism litters their demeanor. They are disconnected not only from themselves, but from any perceived emotional connection, and they pollute the earth with their fractured sense of being. I know of someone just like this. This brand of woman will jump up and down on your heart, clawing at it all the while, ripping it, shredding it, like I saw a blue jay do to a smaller bird of prey in my back yard – up and down, trouncing the poor, helpless, tender creature, stomping the life right out of it, ceasing the flow of blood through its chambers...this is your heart and the blue jay is your shameless girl. And after she's done, she'll have no shame in spitting on your corpse and moving on with her life as though it's all part of the normal protocol.

God is not kind to those who are not kind to others.

-- ARABIAN PROVERB

51. **If she "cuts n' runs" after the first rough patch or period of adversity in the relationship,** (and it wasn't due to something severe like cheating, drug use, criminal behavior or physical, verbal and emotional abuse, in other words, your actions did not merit her reaction) you are so much better off. Let her run, and then you promptly turn around and run the other way – away from her. Allow her to continue running from herself, from you, and from any prospect of happiness that she may now never know as a result of her own spastic idiocy. To cut n' run is 'coward's play'. Relationships require work and communication, and both summarily lead to a more solid and more enduring relationship, thus, her actions are not the least bit admirable. It is a definitive sign of insecurity and indecision, and perhaps an unstable, erratic mind. Women who do this are often lost and misguided.

Do you really want to be with someone like this? She won't even stop to consider the losses – all of the time and moments mutually invested in whatever foundation was created that now must be started again from scratch with

---

Not till we are lost, in other words,
not till we have lost the world, do we begin
to find ourselves, and realize where we are and
the infinite extent of our relations.

-- HENRY DAVID THOREAU

someone else. Thank your lucky stars! It is meant to be that you found out now. You do not pair well with her.

These types of women will be in denial for the rest of their days, carrying baggage that they refuse to face and with which they refuse to reconcile. They can be cold and unapologetic. They can go from loving to loveless in a single day. If you were to demand specific reasons for their running, they will be unable to give them, perhaps only to say, "It's just what I do." They live in a lie, numb to the true jewels of life; experiencing half-emotions that mislead most men. They may think they are in love, but their love is fleeting with little substance because the relationships before you still linger – all of the men before you from whom they cut n' ran and thus, not even *they* know what they feel, or what emotions of love or affection truly feel like, because they can't identify them. They are mere shells of a healthier self.

It is hard to identify these types of women. One sign to look for is whether they seem to continually gloss over reality and coast through moments as if they were on some prolonged opium trip. You may be led to believe that they are laid back and 'really cool' about a lot of issues, when in reality, it may be a complete mask and a sign of their withdrawal. They are simply incapable of a healthy relationship until they stop and examine their own con-

---

The hottest love has the coldest end.

-- SOCRATES

science, and go within and face themselves; until they conduct a thorough self-examination, and you don't want to be around if that happens. So let this description be your explanation for their actions and your closure, and if they try and come back to you, it would have to be after some extensive reassessment on their behalf before you should even consider it, otherwise say, "No, thank you."

A woman who cuts n' runs can leave you feeling a sting of hurt, stealing your ability to trust another and to give of yourself. Be patient and be strong – the pain will pass and someone better and more deserving of you will venture along, into your life.

52. If your mate always wants a world of fantasy and unattainable luxury, lives beyond her means – and yours – and has an illusory outlook on life, always seeing the greener grass elsewhere rather than in you; if she doesn't relish being in your presence and instead discusses those perceptibly "upper-crust" people she fancies, and if she desires more than what you have to offer and goes to extensive measures to suggest or point it out to you, then let them go elsewhere and bid them farewell, unless you are exactly the same way! I should not need to tell you that living this way is not financially sound or advisable, and

---

With all my will, but much against my heart,
We two now part.

-- COVENTRY PATMORE

there is often no emotional investment. Unless you have a dynamite job with a superfluous savings account, you'll be broke by the time the next recession rolls in.

Hers is a variation of the "gold-digger" mentality. She may not be digging for gold, but she wants you to have it and she makes it a point to remind you. Should your money suddenly dry up, she'll be gone with it, and without any remorse for you. Who cares how pretty she is, cut her loose! There has not been one face in the history of the human world that did not wrinkle…unless it's a robot.

53. If she is a control freak – this is an easy one. You either submit to her every desire, request, plan and idea, or the relationship will not last. What do control freaks need? C'mon, this is another easy one…duh? Someone they can control! If you are not a submissive, ambiguous wimp, then you better buy her a pet as a parting gift – something she can control – before telling her to get the hell out of your life, and "Stay out!" The first sign you are with a control freak? When they call *you* one! Why are they accusing you of this? Because they are having difficulty controlling you! You are resistant to their selfish

---

LORD ILLINGWORTH: The Book of Life begins with a man and a woman in a garden.
MRS. ALLONBY: It ends with Revelations

-- Oscar Wilde, A Woman of No Importance

ways. As soon as your partner makes this accusation, your first reaction may be to say "Go F--- yourself!" because they'll find the control that they seek in doing so, but instead, just maintain poise and character and show them the door. It's *CONTROL 101*. If you stay with her, stand aside and watch, while she does all of your planning for you – and I'm talking plans that are years and years in advance. Now THAT'S control! These controlling women are so locked in their own head and desires that they never see you for who you are.

What are some other signs that you might be with a control freak? She nags you. She likes speaking *at* you and *telling* you (and it's not necessarily what to do); she'll make plans months in advance, hold a meeting to tell you the itinerary, and expect you to know exactly what your schedule is, and if you don't, you'd better ask *her*! She'll expect you to plan your day around hers, and if there's a conflict, you'll hear the beast in her roar. She may try to 'train you' by criticizing your habits of leisure and hobbies, in an effort to try to get you to conform to her ways and expectations; she may even find the audacity to tell you to stop participating in those activities that you find enjoyable, stress-relieving and life-diverting, like fantasy

---

Love is the delusion that one
woman differs from another.

-- H.L. MENCKEN

sports or that monthly night of beer and cards with your friends, smoking cigars or playing baseball or softball.

Get rid of these types who want to literally run and *control* your life or they'll be the ruination of your freedom, your friends – and your life. As long as you don't shirk your own responsibilities, she should accept you for who you are, just as you ought to accept her. Attempts made to control people, to try to change them, only leads to misery.

54. If she fails to accept responsibility for her actions, and shoves it all off on you, or even worse, sweeps it all under the rug where it is left to fester with the collected dust, dropped corn flakes and niblets of corn, to be raised at a later date, beware, for you will soon become the excuse and scapegoat for all of the problems that never got resolved – you will be the one blamed for EVERY-THING! Confront her now and if she is volatile and resistant to your attempts to fix the mitigating issues, tell her "goodbye"; if you don't, you'll be left with piles upon piles of unsolved issues, arguments and moments that will collectively amount to a tarnished relationship, dotted and speckled with rancid scents and stale flavors.

Resolve to be thyself; and know that he,
Who finds himself, loses his misery!

Matthew Arnold, Self-Dependence

For some people, unsolved issues mount and mount and build, until one day, they snap, unable to physically cope with the cumulative pressures, upon which it may then become a medical issue. Some say communication is everything, in this instance, it is absolutely true. In an age when social and personal responsibility is waning at an alarming rate, you've *got* to take the time to find someone who is responsible for their own actions – it is imperative for a healthy relationship.

55. If she is never wrong about anything, to an obnoxious degree, and she pointedly tells you that *it's her way or the highway,* tell her "it's over". Get away from her. Unless of course you are so weak-willed you can't stand up for yourself or...you actually enjoy being constantly minimized to a snail in a shell; humiliated and made to believe you don't know a damn thing – for some men humiliation is a 'turn-on'.

These types usually act as though the earth revolves around whatever they say or do. They think they know all there is to know about everything! *Get out of my friggin' life already – you make me sick! You are not as important as you think you are, girl! There are fifty other ways to do the things you do...AND YOU CAN BE WRONG, HAVE*

A fool sees not the same tree that a wise man sees.

-- WILLIAM BLAKE,
The Marriage of Heaven and Hell

BEEN WRONG, AND ARE WRONG FOR ACTING LIKE AN OVERLY STUBBORN, SPOILED, SELF-CENTERED, EGOTISTICAL BITCH! (Sorry, these are my own sentiments. I couldn't control myself.)

These types of women think they are more superior to a walking encyclopedia and Einstein, rolled into one! From suntan lotion to the place to buy the best cuts of meat; to how to cut an apple or the best technology purchase, to the best condoms...you name it, they know it, and good luck convincing them otherwise. When you try to break up with them, they'll probably say, "No, you're wrong," to which you continue waving goodbye and reply, "You combed your hair wrong, your clothes don't match and you have halitosis."

Decisions should be mutual. There should be a 'give and take', as well as flexibility. You may notice that people – both men and women – who think they know everything often demonstrate an extreme lack of empathy, and an overabundance of ego, which just might be a mask for their own inner insecurity. They need something to control and dominate, to give them a sense of purpose. Yes, summarily psychological in nature, but you don't have to deal with it.

———————

Life is a long lesson in humility.

-- JAMES M. BARRIE

56. If she doesn't respect your passions and interests, and shuns your goals and dreams; if they fail to morally support you in your endeavors, even down to the arguments and differences you may have with others, tell her to get the hell out of your life! You might as well be alone! You are not meant to be together with this woman. You will forever argue! She will not be genuinely happy for you when you succeed because she doesn't respect your passions or agree with your cause. Her loss of control of you will become an emotion in her that runs wild. What is the point of staying with her? The sex? To have someone pretty on your shoulder? Sure, she'll keep you in bed for as long as she can because she knows you're not working toward your goals; it is in her best interest to detain you. Wake up! You're wasting your time.

She does not have to agree with you on everything – not even 65% of everything, but if she is adamantly dissuading you from your life's passion and interests, you need to cut her loose and fast – your life is ebbing in her presence. You are simply selling yourself short. Also, you need to know something very, very important, whether you want to read it or not: *Romance can be the stall to all of your dreams, goals and passions.* It is a harsh realization but a true one (for men and women). Relationships require oodles of time and commitment. Jealousy can very

---

Never underestimate the power of human stupidity.

-- ROBERT A. HEINLEIN

often become an issue in her that derails you. She may even give you the dramatic pity play, "I feel like I am on the sidelines of your life". She doesn't support you because your dreams are not about *her*! She cannot respect nor like the fact that you are wholly independent.

My experience has been that many modern women do not like independent men. What's more, many women who say they are "very independent", are not at all. This is another reason why I have great respect for career-minded women who do not waver – they are steadfast in their pursuits and they haven't the time for petty crap like jealousy and envy, and controlling the time it takes you to urinate at a dinner party. In fact, most of these latter types of women will laugh at such outrageous and ridiculous issues.

You need to find a woman who will respect your dreams and be proud of you for all you want to live for – this life should be an adventure, not some safe, risk-less, mundane existence, and you shouldn't be hindered while living it. There is a glut of small-minded people in this world, try not to get stuck with one.

There is a disclaimer to this rule. Be absolutely sure that you are indeed considering your partner in your

---

The sound of a kiss is not so loud as that of cannon, but its echo lasts a great deal longer.

-- OLIVER WENDELL HOLMES, SR.,
Professor at the Breakfast Table

plans; that you are including them in your thoughts and making the effort to *show* them, i.e. short love notes, surprise flowers, and romantic date nights. Do not be selfish. And of course, urge your partner toward their own pursuits, or to take up new ones – and support them! Relationships are about working in concert, and supporting each other's dreams and pursuits. This rule applies to those women who dissuade you from everything you hold dear, and they always leave you fending for yourself; they want *all* of your attention to themselves, without caring for your personal fulfillment. They may also have an interest in controlling you.

57. **If she suddenly starts canceling dates and get-togethers with you, and her actions are completely odd and out of character;** she sends you a text message to cancel a dinner date or leaves you a message on your home phone when you are at work to cancel another engagement or what was supposed to be a quiet night alone. If it is apparent that she is avoiding you – be on your guard, for she may be getting ready to pull out or she is having doubts, or…she may be interested in someone else. Confront her and get to the bottom of it, or tell her you're moving on. If you don't, you better buy a protective

---

All discarded lovers should be given a second chance, but with somebody else.

-- MAE WEST

cover for your heart because it may be on the verge of breaking. It's not about beating her to the punch, but rather about protecting yourself. Such behavior indicates severe instability in your relationship. Just beware.

58. **If your girlfriend is a yeller,** and I don't mean *Old Yeller* – if that was the case, you'd have it easy – I mean, if she yells and screams all the time – *ALL THE TIME*, and it has become clear that she was never taught how to whisper, she knows only one vocal volume, and your neighbors have called the police because they thought someone may be on the verge of being massacred, and you are the total opposite; if your soul is nice and calm and seeks peace – you should probably break up with her. If you don't, you'll be on valiums and an anti-anxiety regimen soon enough, if you are not already. What are you even doing with her? She probably tells you what to do or berates you too, right? She may be a crazy loon...or a soon-to-be crazy loon.

However, she may only yell because she comes from a big family, because those who do come from large families have a propensity to yell, and this does *not* qualify them as a crazy loon – just someone who, YELLS ALL THE

Breaking up is like knocking over a *Coke* machine. You can't do it in one push. You gotta rock it back and forth a few times, and then it goes over.

-- JERRY SEINFELD

TIME! They got used to it growing up, having to yell over all of their siblings just to be heard. But if you're not a yeller, it really can be unpleasant, especially in public places and in an argument. In the latter they would definitely out-yell you, with plenty more yelling in the reserve tank. You may find their yelling endearing – okay. Then live with it. And when you're 90 and she's still yelling, I hope you're still smiling, and still find it endearing.

There are many men who also like to yell; who communicate only through yelling, and if you're one of them, and that is a quality that you seek, well then...I hope you find a yelling mate and you live happily ever after...yelling yourselves into delirium...maybe away from other people, in the woods somewhere...or the forest...where you could scold and yell at *Big Foot* for being on the run all these years. Take a good *Polaroid* for me.

**Love is only half the illusion;
the lover but not his love, is deceived.**

-- GEORGE SANTAYANA

The 'Break-Up' Sample: She's just not who you thought she was

"What do you mean, "it's about the love?""

"I don't know whether I just love you or I'm *in* love with you," she said.

"What! After all this time? So what are we supposed to do, negotiate? Do you need an arbitrator? You're fucking kidding me, right?"

"And there's the issue I have about stability…I may want to stay home when we have kids, and I won't be able to do that on your salary alone."

"That's a low blow. All this time you've known my situation. I told you the day we met what I was able to offer you, and right now, since I'm in grad school, I don't have a lot of money. Now all of a sudden you change your mind? After almost two years you just change your mind?"

"I don't know. I need time."

"We're supposed to get married in four months. I can't believe you're doing this…" He waited for a response, but none came. "Are you going to say something? What's wrong with you?"

"I just can't be here with you right now," she said. Her face was taut and stressed, as if she was on the verge of a break. "I just need space," she said, "a few days."

"You need more than a few days," he said. "What you just said to me and now you can't be here? You want to go and think it over? If you need space then I need the ring back. I'm not going to let you walk out that door, as my fiancée, with my ring still on your finger, and I can't call you…or know when I'm going to see you again. How is that fair…or even logical?"

"Please…" her voice tailed off. She wore an expression indicating a mind that was mentally unreachable.

"No," he said, "give me the ring back. I'm not waiting on the sidelines for you. If you have these issues now, what's it going to be like later? How can I trust you?"

She stood motionless for a long, desolate moment. "Would you have rather I held all this in? That wouldn't have been right –"

"You're only telling me now because I pressed you. I knew something was going through your head, I just didn't know what it was. The way you've been acting…"

"I just need a little time, I don't want it to end this way."

"Nor do I, but too bad. You're already forcing me to end it this way – forcing *us*, acting like a spoiled brat, throwing all this bullshit at me at the last minute. What about the stuff you said on the phone? You're not even thinking about us. Give me the ring back. Fuck this."

She reluctantly slid it off her finger, along with all the love that had ever been between them, and put it on the table. "What did I do to you that was so awful?" he asked. "Why did you suddenly withdraw and turn on me?"

"I don't know," she said, "it's what I do when I have doubts."

"That doesn't make it right," he said, "just going along, glossing over life, and not facing your faults. It makes you a coward. All you know how to do is keep running."

"That's not fair."

"Is this fair to me? You think this doesn't hurt? Or do you even know how to think beyond yourself? You wait until now to decide that I don't make enough money for you? You're a gold digger, just like all the rest. You don't know a damn thing about love. I was willing to make you the happiest wife on earth – whatever it took. You tricked me into thinking you were the one. It was all an act. Do you even realize what we could have had?" he said.

"We still could," she said.

"How? I'm not calling you. You say you need space and all that materialistic stuff you said to me –"

"I'll call you," she said.

"Damn you! All of these issues…they all came from your mother and sister – all of their making, flooding your head with shit, and you know I'm right! How can you listen to them? As if your sister's relationship is any-thing great. They don't know what we had. What about the love that got us here? One rough patch and you cut n' run? Running from yourself because you're letting others cloud your mind! How could you criticize the gifts I gave you? Who fucking does that? I buy you six or seven gifts for Christmas and you criticize one of them! Then you get upset because my parents didn't call you on your birthday, when they just gave you a gift last week and took you out to dinner – this is all petty bullshit! Siding with your mother and creating an issue over my mother's wedding dress that you never laid eyes on; being passive aggressive toward her. . .who ARE you all of a sudden? I can't believe I'm even hearing myself say this! I didn't realize until now how material and fake you really are." He paced the room, running his hand through his hair, his mind spinning. "You just remember that I ran the full race here," he continued, "with my integrity intact. You can't say the same for yourself."

"I'm sorry I can't do this right now. I can't fight with you –"

"I'm not fighting. This isn't fighting. It's anger and sadness. It's closing."

"I don't know what to say. I'm sorry –"

"You're *not* sorry. You don't know where "sorry" begins, and you don't know what to say because you've already said it all and heard it all behind my back – instead of coming to me to communicate, you did it all with your snobby mother and sister, letting them influence your life, scheming and nitpicking me to death. I was in this relationship with them too and for that, thank God, I'm glad it's over." He continued to pace. He didn't even want to look at her, but he knew he had to. "I should have known better. A normal person just doesn't do this – they don't act the way you're acting –"

"Please stop. I can't help the way I feel –"

"You mean the way you *don't* feel…I should have seen this coming and ended it a long time ago. You will never be satisfied in this life, not ever. There will always be a void, and you will always want more. What you need is someone you can control, some rich, submissive wimp who will worship you and only say "yes" while he holds his balls." He finally stopped pacing and forced himself to face her. "Maybe you have your eye on someone else. This is useless. You're so numb right now, but somewhere deep down in your gut you must know that what you're doing isn't right. You *have* to know. Unless your heart is ice cold, which just maybe it is. Thanks for nothing. Now there's the door…goodbye. I have no respect for you anymore… zero." His voice tailed off, his last words coming out of a mouth that quivered in pain.

They faced each other one last time. Then, with tears streaming down both their cheeks he solemnly watched her open his door, step out, and walk to her car. He wondered how there could be a separation if there were mutual tears, mutual sadness – it must mean something. But it only meant an end. He tried to remember what their last kiss felt like, tried to capture the scent of her skin, the hug of her body, their mutual laughter, all of the moments that got them to this point – that were now gone; so close and suddenly so far. He watched her drive away, farther and farther from him, until the taillights disappeared.

When he called to be sure she got home safely, it was the last time he heard her voice. His days persisted, at first slowly, sadly…he could feel the weight of each hour. He felt helpless, riddled with feelings he did not recognize that were alien to him. He tried to figure it all out, but it got him nowhere. He knew he had to forgive her; tell himself to forgive her and forgive himself for his own sorrow and faulty perceptions of a woman who was not who he thought she was; he knew he had to do this to heal and move on. After a few weeks, the sadness started to dissipate. He felt stronger and he gained more strength every time he reminded himself of the reasons they broke up – he knew they were good reasons, until one golden morning, when he awoke to complete renewal. It was just something that happened, like a new season. He could still feel his heart reeling and re-grouping, with an occasional reminiscent pang, but he knew he was going to be okay. All was well.

Just four short months later, he realized it was the best thing that ever happened to him, a fateful force of life; those tears that night were tears of disappointment. He was disappointed in her as a human being, and the tears flowed because of a lost investment, a fruitless pursuit of happiness, but his life had already transformed, like the cells in a body that renew every 90 days, his life was no longer the one that was once existent when he was with her. New habits. New dreams. Fresh days. He slowly reclaimed his life, rediscovering himself and those things dear to him. Four months later…four months wiser, he was eternally grateful that he took the ring back. Time was his ally, and his life, as if a sign from the gods above, had already moved on.

The Resource Pages
You just broke up and your corn flakes are all mushy – your post-game pep-talk

Revelation

While you read the rules in this book, you probably encountered at least one episode or anecdote that fit you, one that related to a circumstance in your relationship – past or present. Thoughts of that significant other no doubt surfaced and cursory language may or may not have risen up from the bowels of your gut, and perhaps even escaped your mouth – hopefully you were aware of who was around you.

*Love, affection, adoration…*they are the temples of the heart, and so often emotions connected to these states of being control our better judgment. The heart hasn't a brain, it knows only how to feel, how to invest itself as soon as it is given "clearance" to do so; how to throw itself head-first into the hopes and comfort and dreams of an ever-after. Because of this, people often stay in relationships too long, gun-shy and afraid to pull the proverbial trigger on the relationship and get out of it, despite the countless signs of present or future anguish staring you in the face; despite the verbal or mental abuse that you may be experiencing; despite the heartlessness of your mate – the perceptible soulless acts of inconsideration…because the heart does not know how to back up – how to go in reverse, unless you order it to, often requiring that you physically pull yourself away from the relationship before you can even begin to pull your heart away. Often times the heart acts on its own volition once it is committed, and thus, it can be said that the heart, when in the throes of a relationship or passionate romance, becomes a wholly separate entity. After any difficult break-up your heart will always remind you when its investment has been lost. For many people – mostly those sincere and honest souls – the heart's main habits are committing, loving and enduring.

The Birth of Relations

The juncture at which a relationship is born…like any birth, it begins with a seed – that tug and squeeze of your gut and the nondescript sensation that showers over your soul, born out of a smitten heart and a mind unable to focus on nothing else but the object of affection, until it is won, like a sport of conquest. If ever there is elation, it is at the onset of love, when affection seems flawless, and perhaps it is – perhaps it *always* is in its infancy, but when the glistening dust settles and the buoyancy dies, what have you? There better be something. In a healthy and sincere relationship, the love just doesn't get up and walk away – it graduates and ripens. Many people lament, "If only the feelings associated with this initial period could last forever!" If only it was like chewing bubble gum, with constant flavor bursts, sumptuous sugar blasts and juicy bubbles that make the glands salivate, however even bubble gum matures and gets old and stale, the decision to throw it away ultimately lying with the person that chews it. The longer the gum is chewed the more difficult it is to work into a bubble. It becomes tough and stiff, but retains its purpose. Ironically, the best bubbles often come when all of the sugar is gone – patience and work rewarded.

Love

Have you paused to ask yourself what it feels like to be in love? Can you describe it in words? Think of the senses of love; the senses involved in love. Does it have a smell? Of perhaps fresh Christmas pine or balsam and fir? Simmering apple-cinnamon cider or an old ball field with its histories of glory? What about heartache? As a heart is breaking, cracking with tears and bursting, revealing fissures, does it give off a scent? Might it smell like fire and soot? Dust from an old, decrepit building? The hot smells of perspired life that rise up through the sidewalk grills, from subway platforms below, on a hot summer day in the city? Or perhaps the disposed yellow coat of a freshly peeled banana, before it becomes disposable waste and fodder for the earth below? Or is it the blood that flows from a rare-cooked filet mignon, that squirts out as the knife cuts through; like the feelings you might get when the words of your ex cut deep ravines through your heart? If so, might new love smell like fresh-cut flowers or a new born baby while seasoned love smells like a fine wine or the prestigious bark of a hundred year-old redwood? To me, love is like good, hearty laughter, abundant, joyful and like each laughing inhale, it feels new and shiny; it is a Bermuda vacation and a head-long dive into a pool of liquid chocolate. True and honest love is like good and constant sex, there is always stimulation. In the concourse of the euphoria that a fresh love emits, we are all hedonists, addicts to its countless pleasures, wanting multiple helpings and hoping the supply never ends.

Think of the cumulative amount of ourselves that we invest in love. What of the individual parts? What would it look like if it was broken down into ingredients or segments and painted on a canvas? What organs in your body feel it the most? The least? Have you actually stopped and examined the physical and emotional senses that you experience, tracing them to their origin, running your finger along them, like a topographic map, to discover where they originate – or where they end? Can you identify your own love and name the parts? How much of yourself do you really know?

In love, the blood seemingly flows with added pep, upon which you experience that rush, and the brief, faint palpitation of your heart that translates into bursts of energy and a feeling. A breadth of emotion runs through you, coloring your anatomy with the nymphs of romance: lust, attraction, affection, wantonness and stimulation. If you can identify and feel this, following its path, then you have the physical proof of your emotional mechanism; proof of your own depths! It is the physiology of love. To recognize this is to better know yourself. It is where your affection resides.

Love, once enacted and released, like a fragrant odor from the heart, initially steals us into a poetic oblivion – it is after the oblivion is over when we learn the fate of our love, affection and relationship; it is after the oblivion when we may start to spot the red flags, potential problem signs that speak first to our subconscious. If the problems become real issues marked with any severity or seriousness, issues that violate our personal constitution, then our conscience is given a swift kick in the butt and a red alert is broadcast to our psyche. This is the alert that needs to be heeded and immediately addressed in order to determine whether action needs to be taken. Ultimately, it will also help you to choose a more compatible mate; this is why it is so important to be in tune with yourself. Instincts rarely lie, for they are sent from your subconscious.

Love is a relative emotion, most everyone has a different interpretation of their supposed love; of their feelings and emotions depending on a large number of factors, i.e. maturity, life circumstances, career, etc., but most everyone does claim or admit to a common aspect of love – a certain level of euphoria that makes them feel perceptibly giddy or drunk; a buoyancy, most notably at the onset, but for some, it can and does last forever. It is when love is at its best, fresh and new, and to know this euphoria is a discovery of the self. Love is a very, very special emotion, one not to be taken frivolously. It is an emotion that can move a whole world and its people, and, on occasion, often does.

In other words, your love is something to be guarded. You must protect it from those mates who might run away with it, abuse it or destroy it, leaving you jaded in the wake. You've got to learn how to find the right partner, or know if you're with the right one. We all have the ability. You must understand yourself in order to apply it.

The 21st century is already seeing a boom in meditation practices, involving Yoga, quantum physics and mechanics, and other spiritual endeavors. We are absolutely in the dawn of a new age; we are living in its beginning ingredients. Participating in some form of meditative exercise is highly advisable, as it helps keep you grounded, and in touch with YOU; what you are feeling – or not – it can help you identify energy blockages and, believe it or not, help decipher those situations that are good for you, and those that are not, ultimately resulting in healthier and more successful relationships, in business, in life, and in love. It will sharpen your instincts and help you to operate with a clear mind, which, in this current world climate, has become a challenge. Remember, if you are not healthy, how can your relationship be healthy? How can your love? You must not be careless with it.

Sustenance (Or Lack Thereof)

Once matured, a relationship is a volley – sometimes for serve. It is inevitable that she will come to expect the back n' forth, the give n' take and the mutual exchange that she may claim she does so well – just as you might, but the reality in your relationship might be that either one or both of you fails to do it at all, and instead, makes a life out of "expectation" and "entitlement". Remember, a relationship is about arriving at a fair and mutually equitable middle ground; strolling down the same path not seeking to change each other, but respecting each other, and growing together.

One afternoon I was at a bar with work colleagues enjoying an end-of-the-week beer, when I overheard one of the women say, "Men are here to entertain me. I want to be entertained. I want them to show me what they've got!" I wanted to puke, take all the wheat and hops and barley I had just consumed, open my mouth and hose her down with it. *Entertain you?* This is to what I was alluding, when, at the beginning of this book I indicated how the male-female playing field – or dating field – is changing. Do you really think an equitable relationship can be had with this woman? I don't think so. I wondered what it must be like living in her head. I concluded that she must run through her days, singing in her mind: *It's all about me! Me! Me!*

There should be reciprocal and mutual decency, courtesy, and consideration in a relationship; there should be equity, but so often, these expectations and standards are not fulfilled, leading to a lopsided struggle of wills, and when a relationship turns sour, it can fast become like dead fish – after a while it stinks up the place!

You are the only keeper of your soul; you must care for it well or risk days of misery, or even something worse than misery. What can be worse than misery you ask? Most people who have been through a divorce will gladly line up and tell you all about it. In our society at present, divorce statistics are already staggering, why add to them? Thus, this book is also about responsibility to *self*, in order to retain a happy soul. If you're in a relationship that lacks equity and stability, one that hasn't any sustenance and is all over the Richter scale with a large dose of tremors, do you think it is healthy to remain in that relationship?

Aspects of Fear

Fear of emotional hurt and loneliness, fear of the unknown, and the loss of fond memories, comfort, and familiarity, are the culprits that only end up prolonging the pain in a bad relationship or making it worse. Invariably, these factors only detain the greater freedom of a healthier self, that great epiphany and life revelation that await you. After all, life is *supposed to be* enjoyable. If you continue to stay with someone who is careless with your heart or someone who is simply wrong for you, only heartache and eventual anger stand in the streets of your tomorrows, waiting to take you up in their clutches. So, why continue to do this to yourself? You must put fear aside. *Fear* is only a prediction, you don't know if the prediction is going to come true unless you face it to find out, upon which, you might ultimately discover your true self. If you take a leap forward in life, you might fall, but how do you know you won't fly?

Have strength and adhere to your personal constitution of what you inherently "know" is right or wrong. If it is a bad situation – a situation that no longer serves your growth and evolution and happiness – then get some balls and tell them "goodbye". If you are not happy then she eventually will not be either. If you wait when you know you shouldn't, you will only be hurt, impeding your life's journey and path. The end of a relationship is much like death, and like death, when the time is up, well…the time is up! Relationships do run a course, like everything else in life. It is part of a cycle, and when the cycle ends, it is a signal to stand up and move on.

Pain? Sure, there will be pain. No ending is pretty or pleasant, that is why it is called "an end", but taking initiative to protect your own heart, because your partner – whether consciously or unconsciously – has opted not to, will eventually empower your resolve. After it is over, you may ask yourself, *why did I have to meet that person or get involved with that person?* Perhaps you needed the experience to make the next one better. Be patient. It may have been an experience for you *and* a lesson for them, or vice versa.

Heartache in the Aftermath

Some people are able to walk away from a relationship without any residual feeling – especially if they have been blessed with a darned good reason or if they are at peace with the finish. In the movie *Heat*, Robert De Niro tells Val Kilmer to "allow nothing to be in your life that you cannot walk out on in 30 seconds flat, if you spot the heat around the corner. " A stark bit of advice. There are many degrees of heartache, some minor and some major. In moderate to severe cases, heartache riles the mind into building its own personal prison, with its own torture chamber of incessant recollection that surpasses with ease any previously held notions of hell. Heartache has but one soldier at its disposal – the mind – that is often without a plan, riddled by the shock and jolt of the moment, too inept from soulful fractures to even raise a sword. And so…all it can do for the heart, is walk…and walk, as far away as possible, pausing now and again to try and shake itself from the rut, in an attempt to shed a little more ache. The mind realizes that time is the only, ever-present, intangible medicine. Space must be put between the ever-progressing present and the ever-wrenching memory of yesterday, until the emergence of a new self that is re-newed and refreshed, like a phoenix rising out from the ashes of its former existence.

In the first eight weeks following a break-up, you may find yourself unenthused about every aspect of life, forced to assume and adopt a new reality; it may be difficult to imagine a way out of your mindful prison, but usually after those first eight weeks you will be out of the woods of hard pain, and after twelve to twenty weeks, a new per-spective sets in – the epic realization of relief, when you wipe your brow and say, "Thank God I'm out of that one!" Be patient. Time really can be your ally if you don't panic. A break-up can feel like a bucket of tiny hearts, all pierced with holes through their chambers. It can be a tattoo of aches decorating the floor boards of a man's soul. Believe me, I know. The psychological effect can be a wallow in a swath of grief that rolls in like a thunderous fog and seeps into the soles of your feet. You must keep your faith and keep looking forward, and use the lessons from the past to excel in the future – but try *not* to look back! As baseball Hall of Fame pitcher Satchel Paige once said, "Don't look back. Something might be gaining on you." It's more good advice.

Sorting it Out

Many of the anecdotes and examples detailed in this book reflect a partner or mate who is careless or derisive, petty-minded or inconsiderate; emotionless or mean, or frankly, a complete and utter jerk! Other examples reflect a partner who may not be the person you thought they were, which can be the most difficult fact to admit – you discover that their heart and soul are emptier than a hole, a cavity of deadened, zombie-like gnomes. Still other examples reflect a mate who is a coward, someone who hides or runs from themselves, afraid to directly confront issues or someone who cannot find the guts to talk to you face-to-face, instead using email or texting to convey confrontational or volatile information and demands (for many in our present society, email and text messaging is a *hiding* tactic). You found episodic anecdotes that reflect someone who is immeasurably selfish and controlling. There are varying degrees of each category or situation, much like the myriad personalities that populate our society. A good portion of the dramatized scenarios contained herein are plucked straight from my personal experiences with past girlfriends and exes, or situations and events that people I know experienced – they are not made up.

At this juncture, I want to give you one rule of caution: Never, *ever* resort to physical violence as a result of any perceptible offense or break-up. If you feel that way, before you do, put your hands in your pockets and walk away. Personally, I have no respect whatsoever for any man who hits a woman. It is cowardly and lacks integrity on every possible level. By all means, resist violence, if you don't, then you belong in jail. Furthermore, why give your partner a reason not to be with you? Why sink downward on the scale of integrity? Be strong and walk away, and cease all contact, you'll feel better you did later. Move on with your life, it is a big world with countless other prospects. Besides, do you really want to be with someone who rouses emotions of violence in you? Life is too short and it only takes one moment to commit a brutal act, and 10 years to life in prison to pay for it. Remember, *karma* is our soul's balance sheet. There's always consequences for harming others, if not in this life, then expect payback in the next. Don't be stupid! If you are a woman-abuser, stop reading right now, stop abusing your girlfriend or partner, and go get help! Please!

The Relationship Slump

So you're in a relationship that has come to feel like you are trudging through sludge. Every morning when you wake up you feel like you haven't slept in a week. The weight in your mind muddles your thoughts and steals your peace, and life seems to be one morbid bastard. Whenever you talk to your significant other or wake up to them or see them in the morning, for some reason you feel a 'heaviness' that mounts. There is staleness in the relations and in your coffee, stagnancy in your communication, perhaps some trepidation to broach certain subjects, and you are at a stalemate. You inherently know that something is not right. Perhaps a part of you feels ignored, or not considered, and maybe she has expressed the same to you. Perhaps your moral character feels violated, and your values compromised. Regardless, you feel awful and unhealthy in the relationship, but it is more comfortable to hang on. You start to think about what it would be like to get out of the relationship; what you would do and how you would go about your days without your current partner. You start to ponder unfulfilled goals and dreams. You have tried to placate some issues and ignore others just to get along, just hoping the problem spots will pass and you say to yourself, *this is part of working through stuff*, but "working through" has morphed into "just going through the motions". As time goes on, you discover a continuance of the problem areas in your relationship, they latch on to every new thought or subject until nothing is ever new anymore. Something continues to be *not right*, and incidents have occurred that eat away at you. The problems graduate, but the relationship still does not. You feel the need to seek counsel from friends or family, and compare other people's relationship notes to your own – you just *have* to ask, "Is this normal?" But you already know the answer and you may want to resist bringing anyone else's opinion into it. The relationship seems to be running out of breath or not running at all.

A relationship is a rhythm. When the rhythm is uneven or broken, life, the mind and one's perceptions are equally uneven and broken, ambling down avenues with half-finished roofs, cars without tires, and houses all painted the same gray color. Numbness sets in. Space becomes crowded. Eyes become parched. Moments become uneasy, but you don't know why, or how, or where to look, or how to fix it or make it stop. You are lost in the complexity and puzzlement of the human condition; rationale has gone awry, you try to figure it out, but you are not certain where or what to dissect and analyze. There are offenses. That much you do know. It is all you need to know. The question is: How large is the offense? Is it large enough to tell your significant other to get the hell out of your life? Such an act requires courage, but the rest of your life is a long time, and it deserves that courage, as does your heart.

So what do you do? You may need to do the thing that is best – and only you can know what that is, perhaps after reading this book and thinking it through – while being true to yourself and your partner. Maybe you've already done it and you are reading this book for reassurance or as a reinforcement and knowledge for your next relationship. While you think things through, you should have consideration for your partner's life too. If the relationship isn't working; if it's no longer fun, and the spark is gone, and no lengthy communication can fix it, then splitting up is probably best for *both* of you.

If you were in such a situation and if you did just break up with your partner, remember, all pain, grief, heartache and sadness is temporary. It will pass. In time and with a bit of effort on your part, it *will* pass! If you thought you had love in the relationship, think about how much better it will be when the 'right one' comes along.

After the Break

Okay, let's say you just broke up with your significant other/girlfriend/partner. What do you do now? Life! You do *life*! Live! The beat goes on. Go see a movie by yourself – one that is glorious or uplifting or action-packed with thrill, to give your mind a vacation. Go on a cruise. Go on a trip overseas. Read a good book. Go to a sports bar or a good bookstore. Join a social group. Go on a road trip – if you have a dog even better. Hell, go buy a dog! Get together with friends, but you should *avoid* excessive consumption of alcohol – human history has already shown us, on innumerable occasions, that it can have very negative and adverse results, especially when mending from a potential heartbreak. Can you remember how you were the last time you were drunk, if you ever were? Exactly! That's my point! If you can remember, you will recall your mood or the foolish things you did or said, and if you can't remember…that's reason enough to avoid alcohol. Besides, alcohol is a depressant, and if you're already feeling low, a few drops of alcohol could have you digging so deep that you come out on the other end of the earth, in China! In a Chinese laundry eating egg-drop soup and aspirin! You will feel much better if you simply avoid alcohol and other depressants altogether during these post break-up times. Basically, you want to aim to be kind to your heart, and be good to yourself.

You should have your work to keep you busy; your hobbies, your interests, and your life…the world! Go explore it! And don't waste time beating yourself up or fall into the trap of feeling sorry for yourself or rehashing and reminiscing, over-analyzing moments that could have been different – they were not different, she is who she is and they happened the way they did. Period! Do not make it something it never was. Excessive analysis, besides for the sake of self-improvement, can be a moot and damaging process, making your head feel like a roller coaster. What you experienced was not a failure. It is simply part of your journey on this crazy planet; part of your learning curve. You don't deserve any form of misery or disgruntlement. You deserve to be happy.

If she broke up with you…so what! Would you really want to be with someone who doesn't want to be in the relationship? You will not find happiness with someone who wants to leave nor always has their mind on leaving – it is clear you are on different planes of thought – release her, both from your mind and your life. Relationships should not require convincing. Decisions to stay together should be arrived at and felt from within – you just *know*, and if and when it is time to separate, you will know that too! *Choose* to seek and live in a vibration of happiness and wellness, in your relationships, *and* in every other area of life.

Love and relationships are synonymous, kindred experiences. They are both gambles that involve your heart and soul, but they are also brave and admirable, and thus, regardless of the outcome, they are rewarding and part of the beautiful, wondrous intricacies of life. They are risks of the self, the exposure of the innermost part of you. In a broken relationship the hardest part to accept is when you have to reel in all that you ever invested, divulged and revealed, like reeling in a fishing line after a cast, your emotions and a bloody heart dangling from the hook, along with all of those moments you once thought were so meaningful. A broken relationship is a breaking of a habit and the loss of a friend all at once, but you must continue to remind yourself that it is a break for the best – otherwise it probably wouldn't have happened. Take solace in the fact that millions of lives and souls throughout the course of time, long before you, have experienced and endured the same – you are *never* alone! Broken hearts litter the landscape of the human existence – it is part of living and growing, both spiritually and within the maturation process. Extract strength from this realization and move forward. So much awaits you!

This is your life. Now seize it! While no one is perfect, there is nothing wrong with trying to find someone who *is* perfect for *you*! A greater empowerment and a better love await you in the hours ahead. One grand day with the right love erases years of days with the wrong one.

The Rule Recap

1. If she cheats on you.

2. If she tries to entrap you.

3. If your mate has a chemical imbalance and is on prescribed medication, and she did not tell you about it.

4. If your mate craves status or comes from a status-driven family.

5. If she spends your money faster than you do.

6. If your mate is a "gold digger".

7. If you give your girlfriend flowers and she puts them aside with flagrant, unappreciative carelessness.

8. If she misses your birthday and flat out fails to acknowledge it.

9. If she steals from you.

10. If she does drugs and you do not.

11. If she is an excessively jealous person.

12. If your significant other embarrasses you or 'cuts you down' in front of others.

13. If your mate continuously nags you despite your requests to stop.

14. If she frequently exhibits bizarre behavior.

15. If your significant other is emotionally unstable.

16. If she confronts you with issues that are absolutely off the wall.

17. If she insults you and degrades who you are.

18. If she is overly flirtatious with your friends or other arbitrary men.

19. If your mate is making a pointed habit of kissing work colleagues on the lips.

20. If your partner is passive aggressive.

21. If your mate is disrespectful to your parents for no apparent reason.

22. If your mate is utterly absurd!

23. If she deceives you in any way, look out!

24. If your significant other has a meddling mother who sticks her nose in the relationship and all affairs concerning the relationship.

25. The 'Bitch Factor'.

26. If your mate is compulsive liar.

27. If your significant other calls you or text messages you every 20 minutes while you're at work.

28. If your significant other has you followed.

29. If you have a partner who is only in the relationship for her own advantage.

30. If your partner is unable to make key decisions on her own.

31. If she abuses your loyalty and love.

32. If your mate pays little or no attention to you or frequently ignores you.

33. If she bitches and bitches and bitches.

34. If she is never happy with you, no matter how much you do for her.

35. If you suspect she might be gay when you're straighter than a speeding bullet.

36. If you discover that your significant other has been maintaining a "hidden" or ulterior lifestyle – a double life – and she either kept it from you for an extended time or you found out by accident.

37. If you are treated like some career trophy or an equestrian stud.

38. If the formalities of a wedding trump, supersede or overrule your relationship.

39. If you feel like you keep getting "interviewed."

40. If she suddenly stops living the life that you thought (and she professed) defined her.

41. If you already know that her mother is a gossipy, "talk-behind-your-back", "scheme-behind-your-back", status-driven annoyance in your relationship.

42. If she complains about the sex.

43. If she wants to see a relationship counselor before you are even married.

44. If your partner often has violent episodes or resorts to them during arguments.

45. If she is verbally abusive, especially in front of others.

46. If you accidentally (but on purpose) stumble into her email account and find a host of flirtatious emails from wooing, would-be suitors.

47. If she only wants to make a purchase or a life-altering move out of vogue or solely for the sake of image.

48. If she is overly concerned with how much money you earn.

49. If your partner's family is unforgiving, cruel and bullying.

50. If she consistently shows no shame, no morals, no virtue, no couth, and no hesitancy in incurring hurtful blows to you and others.

51. If she "cuts n' runs" after the first rough patch or period of adversity in the relationship.

52. If your mate always wants a world of fantasy and unattainable luxury.

53. If she is a control freak – this is an easy one.

54. If she fails to accept responsibility for her actions, and shoves it all off on you.

55. If she is never wrong about anything, to an obnoxious degree, and she pointedly tells you that *it's her way or the highway.*

56. If she doesn't respect your passions and interests, and shuns your goals and dreams.

57. If she suddenly starts cancelling dates and get-togethers with you, and her actions are completely odd and out of character.

58. If your girlfriend is a yeller.

** Please refer to each individual rule within the book for a more detailed and thorough explanation.

A Guy's Quick Guide
to How to Treat a Woman
– A Top Ten List –

Here is a shortlist of things to do and maintain in order to have and keep a healthy relationship, assuming the efforts are mutual. I will reiterate that a relationship is a two-way street.

1. Empathy! Empathy! Empathy! Don't know what the word means? Then you probably don't practice it enough. Put yourself in their shoes; consider how they might feel about a given circumstance or situation. How might your actions or words affect them? If they are sad from perhaps a loss of family or dejected over a job loss or career demotion, you've got to be sensitive to that. Be sensitive to *them*.

2. Be Honest! You want them to be honest with you, don't you? Do not be careless with the hearts of others or lead them astray – be honest about your emotions. If you fail to see a future with her, then you have a responsibility to tell her; if you're not sure, you'd best try and find your surety as soon as possible. I know inside of the relationship they may get mad at you if you tell them they've gained weight or if you think a certain dress they bought just doesn't look good, but in the end, they should appreciate you for your honesty. Besides, most women wouldn't hesitate to tell you if you're fat or what you're wearing doesn't look good.

3. Ask How Their Day Went. Showing interest and consideration for their daily lives shows that you care, and also, it's just a nice thing to do! Be nice.

4. Break up Before You Cheat! Respect them enough to break up before you are unfaithful. So many people are cheating today, it's just wrong. In fact, it's happening on such a large scale that it is becoming an epidemic of social irresponsibility, as it systemically hastens the erosion of trust and sincerity in our society. I don't know how people who cheat live with themselves, because they live a lie. Would you want it done to you? This falls under the *TREAT PEOPLE AS YOU WOULD WANT TO BE TREATED CATEGORY.* Act with integrity and decency – it's always the best recipe. Come clean, be a man and admit it. And if you ARE going to cheat, you had better have thought it through, because when/if she finds out, she's most likely gone from your life, and I don't blame her!

5. Hold and Open Doors for Them. Have some manners and class, even though we are in an age when it seems everyone has less and less. Don't stop being gallant and chivalrous. Don't know what those words mean? Look them up! If you are constantly being a gentleman in the relationship, what faults will you have? You will always know that you put that proverbial best foot forward – and if she steps on it, then maybe she's not the one, and she fits into one of the rules in this book, in which case, go back and read the rules! Also, *walk* with your woman. Don't walk ahead of her, or behind her, walk *with* her when you are going somewhere together.

6. Shower Them With Occasional Surprises. Flowers. Roses. Earrings. An appointment at a day spa. A card – even an e-card. Dine out. Clean the house. Buy her that coat she wants. Get creative and illustrate a card that is good for 1000 kisses or 500 hugs. A morning love note in her purse or on the dash of her car. Use your imagination…it can get really fun – as long as she appreciates it. And if not…you know what to do!

7. Don't Quit on the Relationship. Meet them halfway. Show interest in them. The best tip I have for maintaining interest and keeping your love fresh and vibrant: Don't stop investing yourself in her or the relationship. Continue to buy her flowers for no reason at all; surprise them with a kiss in an unexpected time or in an unexpected place; be willing to please her with that trip to visit her parents (at least once in a while). Take her to Sunday

Brunch before the 1:00 football kick-off. Again…use your imagination, and if you think yours isn't good, it does get better with practice! So start imagining!

8. Give Them Compliments. No, I don't mean every hour of every day. Just try and do it spontaneously. Do it before you walk out the door to go to dinner; on your way to a family function; when she wakes up in the morning or comes home from work. Tell her that the dress she's wearing looks stunning or her hair looks pretty or she has a smile that can move the heavens and a laugh that can move the earth. Tell her she's so damn beautiful! Do I need to list anymore examples, or do you think you can take it from here?

9. Say "I'm Sorry" When it's Your Fault. If you might one day blame her for not taking responsibility for her own actions, you had better be taking responsibility for yours all along. Also, that one word, "sorry", can tear down *sooo* many walls! It can open the flood gates of communication and mend all your broken relationship fences. The word can have some serious power, just be certain to say it like you mean it, and hopefully you do. Through the course of time, "sorry" has also been responsible for initiating some serious lovemaking sessions! How's that for incentive?

10. Respect Their Passions and Careers. This one is easy: Don't be a bonehead and yell at them or get upset because they are late for dinner because of their job or career demand or pursuit – so long as you're certain that's the reason they are late! Patience and understanding are very important in relationships, exercise them. You don't 'own' your partner. She is not your possession. Have regard for her goals and support her aspirations, and if you don't, you're a jerk. You want her to respect and support passions that you pursue, right? Remember, relationships are two-way streets. Meet her in the middle, and if she is sincere too, bliss shall come.

Bonus Rule: Every Night Before You Go to Bed or Drift to Sleep, Give Them a Kiss! Do it because you appreciate her beside you. It will also help to extinguish any lingering anger or resentment from the day; it shows your love, care or concern for the relationship, and indicates you are willing to take the high road, leapfrogging any of the issues that may be riddling your relations; it shows that you will not let ANY issue get in-between the love or affection you have for her. Even if it kills you, do it! Unless of course you're on the verge of telling her that *you are so done with her!*

About the Author

Liam Carson holds a Master's Degree in Education, and a Bachelor's Degree in Communications. He has had extensive experience in the arena of male-female relations. Liam is a defender of both sexes, especially women's rights. He is a staunch believer in the theory of relativity, and its applicability to all areas of life. His ultimate wish is to create a world of harmony, one in which everybody gets along.

In his spare time, Liam is a fitness enthusiast, martial artist, student of the mind, and taster of wine – the latter of which he likes full-bodied and red, with long legs.